MANAGING GOOD GOVERNANCE IN HIGHER EDUCATION

MANAGING GOOD GOVERNANCE IN HIGHER EDUCATION

Michael Shattock

Open University Press

Open University Press
McGraw-Hill Education
McGraw-Hill House
Shoppenhangers Road
Maidenhead
Berkshire
England
SL6 2QL

email: enquiries@openup.co.uk
world wide web: www.openup.co.uk

and Two Penn Plaza, New York, NY 10121–2289, USA

First published 2006

A catalogue record of this book is available from the British Library

ISBN 10: 0 335 21666 8 (pb) 0 335 21667 6 (hb)
ISBN 13: 978 0 335 21666 6 (pb) 978 0 335 21667 3 (hb)

Library of Congress Cataloguing-in-Publication Data
CIP data applied for

Typeset by YHT Ltd, London
Printed in the UK by Bell & Bain Ltd, Glasgow

CONTENTS

SERIES EDITORS' INTRODUCTION

Post-secondary educational institutions can be viewed from a variety of different perspectives. For most of the students and staff who work in them they are centres of learning and teaching in which the participants are there by choice and consequently, by and large, work very hard. Research has always been important in some higher education institutions (HEIs), but in recent years this emphasis has grown, and what for many was a great pleasure and, indeed, a treat, is becoming more of a threat and an insatiable performance indicator, which just has to be met. Maintaining the correct balance between quality research and learning/teaching, while the unit of resource, at best, holds steady, is one of the key issues facing us all. Educational institutions as work places must be positive and not negative environments.

From another aspect, post-secondary educational institutions are clearly communities, functioning to all intents and purposes like small towns and internally requiring and providing a similar range of services, while also having very specialist needs. From yet another, they are seen as external suppliers of services to industry, commerce and the professions. These 'customers' receive, *inter alia*: a continuing flow of well-qualified, fresh graduates with transferable skills; part-time and short course study opportunities through which to develop existing employees; consultancy services to solve problems and help expand business; and research and development support to create new breakthroughs. It is an unwise UK educational institution which ignores this aspect, which is now given a very high priority by the UK Government.

However, educational institutions are also significant businesses in their own right. One recent study shows that higher education institutions alone are worth £35 billion a year to the UK economy. Moreover, they create more than 562,000 full-time equivalent jobs either through direct employment or 'knock-on' effects. This is equivalent to 2.7 per cent of the UK workforce. In addition, it has recently been realized that UK higher education (HE) is a major export industry with the added benefit of long-term financial and political returns. If the UK further education sector is also added to this equation, then the economic impact of post-secondary education is of truly startling proportions.

Whatever perspective you take, it is obvious that educational institutions require managing and, consequently, this series has been produced to facilitate that end. The editors have striven to identify authors who are distinguished practitioners in their own right and, indeed, can also write. The authors have been given the challenge of producing essentially practical handbooks, which combine appropriate theory and contextual material with many examples of good practice and guidance.

The topics chosen are both of key importance to educational management and stand at the forefront of current debate. Some of these topics have never been covered in depth before and all of them are equally applicable to further as well as higher education. The editors are firmly of the belief that the UK distinction between these sectors will continue to blur and will be replaced, as in many other countries, by a continuum where the management issues are entirely common.

For more than two decades, both of the editors were involved with a management development programme for senior staff from HEIs throughout the world. Every year the participants quickly learnt that we share the same problems and that similar solutions are normally applicable. Political and cultural differences may on occasion be important, but are often no more than an overlying veneer. Hence, this series will be of considerable relevance and value to post-secondary educational managers in many countries.

Thus far, the excellent volumes in this series have concentrated on clear aspects of management. This book by Mike Shattock (and both of the editors feel that we can address him by the familiar diminutive because our early careers were irrevocably shaped by his wide-ranging knowledge and expertise of HE) redresses the balance and deepens the analogies with both businesses and communities by introducing the essential concept of 'governance'. In truth, it is probable that most HE employees will know little, if anything, about their institution's governance arrangements and few outside of the institution will even be aware that they exist. And yet these arrangements have always been very important and, in recent years, have become even more so, especially in the light of the Cadbury, Jarratt and Hampel Reports.

Unfortunately, governance, like management, can be done well or badly and Mike's work provides informative examples of both. Good governance is 'shared governance' and requires good management. This book will go far towards helping to achieve this throughout HE.

David Warner
David Palfreyman

FOREWORD

This book tries to do two things: to describe how university governance has changed and developed over the last quarter of a century (Chapters 2 to 5) and to help those actively engaged in university governance to manage the increasingly complex issues that confront them (Chapters 6 to 8). It is more than 30 years since Graeme Moodie and Rowland Eustace published their classic text *Power and Authority in British Universities* (Moodie and Eustace 1974) and much has changed since then. Sadly, Rowland Eustace, a very dear and valued friend, is no longer with us; he would, I think, have been astonished at how some of the assumptions implicit in that book have been overturned. I wish to acknowledge the debt that anyone writing about university governance now owes to Graeme Moodie and Rowland Eustace's work. *Managing Good Governance* is not written specifically to update *Power and Authority in British Universities* but it is in fact the first full-length text on university governance as a total system to be published since theirs and does seek to show how the pressures of the times have altered the world about which they wrote.

But if one aim of the book is to create an understanding of how the times have changed, another is to offer practical help to those responsible for governance in universities at all levels, from members of governing bodies to participants in academic governance at senates and academic boards, in faculty boards and in schools and departments, and to vice-chancellors, registrars, pro-vice-chancellors, deans and heads of departments and to secretaries of university committees wherever those committees sit in a university governance hierarchy. As a participant myself in the resolution of some of the issues described in Chapters 6 and 7 and as the main author of the first three issues of the Committee of University Chairmen's *Guides on Governance*, I am very conscious of the difficulty of adopting the appropriate governance steps as challenging events unfold quickly around one. The accounts of problems and issues in university governance, and the discussion of the processes and decisions involved, are intended to demonstrate how complex and multi-faceted such matters may be. As universities move increasingly into a more and more marketized environment governance issues are likely to become more important, and their effective management will be more central to the maintenance of institutional stability; good governance will increasingly be regarded as having a major influence on institutional standing and reputation. This book is intended to show that university governance is not simply an academic field of study but has practical and professional lessons to teach about the maintenance of institutional integrity and effectiveness.

I should like to acknowledge a debt of gratitude to a number of people, first to my former colleagues, David Warner and David Palfreyman, for their invitation to undertake the book and their encouragement through its gestation; second to the participants in the Governance module of the MBA in Higher Education Management at the Institute of Education whose intellectual vigour ensured that I have remained continuously engaged with the developing field of university governance since the MBA programme began; and finally, to Cathy Charlton, University Secretary at Warwick, whose astute and helpful comments on the manuscript have greatly improved it. Final responsibility for facts and opinions must, of course, rest with the author.

Michael Shattock

ABBREVIATIONS

AAUP	American Association of University Professors
AHUA	Association of Heads of University Administration
CUC	Committee of University Chairmen
CVCP	Committee of Vice-Chancellors and Principals
DES	Department of Education and Science
DTI	Department of Trade and Industry
HEC	Higher Education Corporation
HEFCE	Higher Education Funding Council for England
HEI	higher education institution
HEQC	Higher Education Quality Council
IT	information technology
NAO	National Audit Office
QAA	Quality Assurance Agency for Higher Education
SEC	US Securities and Exchange Commission
SORP	Statement of Recommended Accounting Practice
TQA	teacher quality assessment
UGC	University Grants Committee
UMG	University Management Group

1

INTRODUCTION

Interest in university governance is of long standing. In 1213, the chancellor issued a Magna Charter of the University in Paris, confirmed by the Pope in 1231, that he was obliged to obtain the vote of professors in matters connected with appointments for the teaching of theology and canon law (Ruegg 1992). Nearly 800 years later university governance remains a contested subject and one which is still evolving to fit a changing environment as much in the UK as in continental Europe (Braun and Merrien 1999). Definitions of governance vary according to context but in universities, and in this book, university governance is defined as the constitutional forms and processes through which universities govern their affairs. As we shall see, governance and management, while theoretically separate functions, have close interrelationships in the university context in a way that is not paralleled in corporate governance generally because governance operates at many more levels in a university setting than would be the case in a traditional company or non-profit organizational structure. There has been a tendency, especially since the 1992 Further and Higher Education Act, to regard university governance in a not dissimilar way, as one would corporate governance in a company setting, as being primarily a question of the way governing bodies operate (cf. Bargh, Scott and Smith 1996), a perception reinforced by the regular issues of updates to the *Guides on Governance* issued by the Committee of University Chairmen (CUC 1995, 1998, 2000, 2004). This book, on the other hand, treats governance as extending right through the institution from a governing body, down through senates and academic boards to faculty boards and departmental meetings and it regards governance as being effective when these levels of governance work together productively. If we believe that teaching and research is the core business of universities (Shattock 2003a) we have to believe that the organs of governance which coordinate, incentivize and sometimes direct these activities carry equal weight in the governance of the institution as a whole even if they may not have the final decision on fundamental strategic and financial issues. This might lead us to see university governance, not from the top on the basis of who governs who, but as part of the organizational law of the institution, a concept defined by Kwickers as:

The administrative, economical and juridical aspects of:

- how an organisation – public or private – is internally structured and governed;
- how it develops strategy and policy and translates these into action;
- how it is legally embedded in its working environment and/or its operational systems;
- how it cooperates with external parties.

(Kwickers 2005)

Organizational governance has become of much more interest in recent years – in higher education as much as in companies and charitable bodies. Two main theoretical approaches to considering governance issues have been developed, agency theory and stewardship theory. Considering university governance through the lens of these different approaches offers interesting perspectives on how universities order their affairs but in neither of them is a perfect fit apparent. Thus agency theory, developed primarily in relation to corporate governance in companies, assumes that owners or shareholders have essentially different interests to those of managers so that the main function of the board is to control and direct the business to ensure that management acts in the best interests of the shareholders and is compliant with board policies (Keasey, Thompson and Wright 1997). Universities do not, of course, have owners or shareholders in this sense, and while in some higher education institutions (HEIs) there might be some tendency for governing bodies to see themselves as being like company boards (some post-1992 universities in London technically have company status and company boards) but even in these cases there are nevertheless strong countervailing constitutional arguments in the existence of academic boards which contradict the analogy. While all governing bodies are made to feel accountable in a financial sense for the expenditure of public moneys, they are not answerable to Government or to a Higher Education Funding Council for the performance of their institution; they occupy the position much more analogous to that of trustees of a charitable organization. HEIs do not have the 'principal' that agency theory demands. But agency theory is not applicable for another reason because most universities do not have 'managers' in the sense that agency theory requires; even in the most 'managerialist' institution the academic community operates within standards of personal autonomy and a diversity of objectives which contradict any notion of a coherent management perspective.

Stewardship theory, which is more relevant to the non-profit sector, also falls short of providing a framework for considering university governance issues. This approach assumes that managers want to do a good job and will act as effective stewards of the organization's resources and the main function of the board is strategic rather than achieving compliance (Muth and Donaldson 1998). While this is more sympathetic to the position of university staff than agency theory it nevertheless fails to capture the role of governing bodies (see Chapter 4), takes no account of the legal and constitutional provisions for academic governance and confines the role of 'managers' (however defined) much more narrowly than is appropriate for the academic community.

It is not surprising that institutions which have as their legally defined object 'the advancement of learning' (Chesterman 1979) do not fit comfortably within theories of governance designed around other organizations, although much modern thinking about governing bodies seems to imply a strong attachment to agency theory approaches (Buckland 2004). The last decade has seen universities placed under enormous pressures of financial stringency, growth and government intervention and it is not surprising that university governance has been subject to criticism and has had to adapt. The actual forms of university governance have, as a matter of history, evolved in various ways since the creation of the civic universities at the beginning of the last century and are continuing to do so. Any book about university governance and how it can best be managed can do no more, in a volatile period of state–university relations, than capture the position of the moment and show how it has been arrived at. On the other hand, there perhaps are some verities, some underlying characteristics of university governance, which mark it out from other forms of governance. These derive from the multi-product character of universities themselves – as teaching institutions at so many levels, as centres of research, including research which has relatively immediate expectations of being of economic utility, and as sites of learning, that is as institutions which, because of the way resources and knowledge workers are brought together within them, have become key contributors to the knowledge society. Governing bodies therefore have an important role, not just in ensuring accountability for government funds but in keeping universities responsive to the wider interests of society. At the same time the critical principle of 'shared governance' needs to be maintained. Kerr and Glade in their influential review of boards of trustees in the US, *The Guardians* (1989), while resisting academic or student representation of boards, recommended that boards should clarify their policies on shared governance taking account of the recommendations of the American Association of University Professors (AAUP) and that

> boards should carefully consider how the faculty can become responsible and reliable partners in the decision-making process.
> (Kerr and Glade *ibid* a)

In Britain academic and student representation on governing bodies are a given, although the level of academic representation differs significantly between the pre- and post-1992 universities, but shared governance goes beyond this to the framework within which strategic decision-making is made and the extent to which the faculty feel engaged with institutional objectives (Shattock 2002). Managing good governance in a university setting means ensuring that governance at all levels in the institution works well, that all the interlocking parts connect smoothly and that the processes combine to deliver an organizational culture which is robust, flexible and willing to take decisions on trust where pressures of timing demand it.

2

THE ORIGINS AND DEVELOPMENT OF MODERN UNIVERSITY GOVERNANCE

The forms of university governance in the UK do not spring from a single tradition as they do, for example, in the US or in most Commonwealth countries. In the UK there is the distinctive Oxbridge model, the mediaeval (or 'ancient' as it is now called in Scotland) Scottish model, the civic university model and the post-1992 higher education corporation (HEC) model. These separate models, although somewhat modified in modern practice, render generalizations about the structure of UK university governance dangerous and the current fashion for Governance Codes, as exemplified in the Lambert and CUC Codes (Lambert 2003, CUC 2004) as simplistic and not to be relied upon because they attempt to smooth over real differences in constitutional machinery that are enshrined in legal forms such as charters and statutes or articles of governance.

The Oxbridge governance model

The Oxbridge model represents the clearest expression of the primacy of academic self-governance essentially because it was derived from the mediaeval concept of a guild of masters recognized by the Pope as an academic corporation of higher learning (Duryea 2000). In Paris, unlike the governance of the University of Bologna, which remained in the hands of the students, the masters achieved corporate status as an *universitas* and were recognized by both clerical authority, in the shape of the Pope, and by the king, as a *studium generale*. By the thirteenth century they were represented by a rector in dealing with external authorities. This structure was in effect exported to Oxford and thence to Cambridge. Indeed, Rashdall argues that 'intercourse between Paris and Oxford was so close that every fresh development of corporate activity on the part of the masters of Paris was more or less faithfully imitated or reproduced at Oxford' (Rashdall 1936 III 49). Both Oxford and Cambridge enjoyed good relations with their bishops (Lincoln and Ely) who retained the right to appoint their chancellors but by the end of the Middle Ages both universities had freed themselves of episcopal jurisdiction and the chancellor became an honorary figure based at the royal court, and a vice-chancellor, elected from within the university, became the effective leader of the university. By the reign of Henry VIII common law permitted a corporation to have the powers of a legal person and the university could hold a seal for the transaction of business, hold property, employ staff and could sue and be sued, rights that remain embedded in the charters and statutes of all the pre-1992 universities, as being held by the university itself rather than by one element in the governance structure, the board of governors, as in the polytechnics and the post-1992 higher education corporations.

However, Parliamentary legislation in 1854 (Oxford) and 1856 (Cambridge), while it reformed the organs of governance to weaken the role of the heads of houses, did not introduce the involvement of laymen (technically, non-ecclesiastical staff) into the governance of the universities and reinforced the role of the academic community through the Hebdomadal Council (Oxford) and the Council of the Senate (Cambridge). (The governance of Trinity College, Dublin, which was founded in 1591, was conceived on the same principles and is similarly different from the constitutions of other universities in Ireland.) Both universities were criticized by the Robbins Report for the complexity of their governance structures and the effect this had on their decision-making processes and both have taken steps through major internal governance reviews conducted by the Franks Committee (University of Oxford 1964a) and the North Committee (University of Oxford 1997) in the case of Oxford, and the Wass Committee (University of Cambridge 1989) in the case of Cambridge, to introduce reforms. Oxford has made significant steps to streamline its structures and has introduced some lay members into its governing body. Cambridge, on the other hand, has rejected a proposal to appoint lay members, including a lay member to chair its council, and has retained the Regent House, which comprises the whole academic staff of the University, as its supreme governing body.

The Scottish governance model ■

The Scottish model which applies in four universities, Aberdeen, Edinburgh, Glasgow and St. Andrews, founded in the fifteenth and sixteenth centuries, followed a different pattern. Again Paris was the inspiration of the founding of the first Scottish university, St. Andrews, and a charter was obtained from the Pope, as at Oxford and Cambridge, although a later revision of its academic governance owed more to the University of Cologne (Green 1969). Glasgow, when the Pope approved the establishment of a *studium generale*, received the privileges and exemptions enjoyed by the members of Bologna University, but its constitution, and Aberdeen's, was closely modeled on St. Andrews. A rector, nominated by officers of the 'nations' into which the universities were divided, had considerable judicial and disciplinary powers but was subject to a chancellor appointed by the relevant bishop, while the teaching masters were organized into faculties led by deans. All three universities became answerable to the Scottish Kirk after the Reformation.

Edinburgh, on the other hand, founded in the late sixteenth century was answerable, through its *senatus academicus*, to the town council which had brought it into existence. Disputes in the nineteenth century between the University and the town council over the University's legal autonomy to make appointments and curricular changes prompted the *senatus* to petition the Home Secretary who established a royal commission to look into the condition of the Scottish universities. In 1858 this resulted in a Universities (Scotland) Act which established a set of commissioners who remodelled all the Scottish universities' governance, introducing a court to each university on which there was to be a majority of laymen and transferring to this body from the senates all those powers which were not specifically the concern of the faculties. This represented a radical shift of power away from the academic community. The rector became an elected position by the students (a remnant of the Bologna connection) and formally chair of the court, while each university was to be headed by a principal (Green *ibid*). These provisions have remained to this day.

Over time the position of the rector in relation to the court has become increasingly anomalous. Traditionally, rectors have chosen not to exercise their right to chair the court (a notable exception being the present Chancellor of the Exchequer, Gordon Brown, when, as a postgraduate student, he was elected the University's rector at Edinburgh). In the absence of the rector the principal chaired the court, but since the late 1980s it has been normal for one of the lay members to be elected to exercise the function of chair. In spite of representations, the Scottish Parliament in a recent review of Scottish higher education chose not to remove the right of a rector to exercise the role of chairing meetings of the court (Scottish Executive 2003). A further consequence of the 1858 legislation was that the separation of powers between courts and senates was much more clear cut than in the later English civic universities, with financial and resource allocation powers exercised exclusively by the courts without any necessary influence by the senates. So separate were the two bodies at Glasgow that the University Secretary only attended senate meetings on the invitation of the senate, meeting by meeting, and to this day a professor serves formally as the clerk to the senate, with a professional university administrator assisting in the practical arrangements. Another notable feature is that the composition of the courts of the ancient Scottish universities are prescribed by the Universities (Scotland) Act 1966 which provides for assessors rather than representative members from various local and regional bodies and are smaller than the councils of their English university counterparts. These constitutional arrangements were not, however, extended to later foundations: Strathclyde and Stirling Universities, which received their charters in the 1960s, were given governance arrangements much more like the institutions founded contemporaneously in England; similarly, the post-1992 universities in Scotland followed the same model as the post-1992 universities in England and Wales.

The civic university governance model

Until 1872 admission to Oxford and Cambridge was restricted to members of the Church of England, and most college fellows were ordained. Moodie and Eustace (1974) speculate that it was for this reason that the University of London, established in 1826 (which was to become University College when a new University of London was established embracing Kings College) appears to have excluded academics altogether from the governance of the institution, a situation repeated in the first statutes of Lampeter and Durham. Indeed, in University College, staff were formally only permitted to communicate with the governors (the Proprietors) in writing, although by 1832 an academic senate was established, by internal regulation, albeit with a lay chairman (Moodie and Eustace *ibid*). The true beginning of the English bicameral system, which constitutes our third model, was in the constitution drafted in 1880 for Owens College, Manchester, where the system of a court as the overall governing body, a council as the executive governing body (and operating like the court of a Scottish university) and an academic senate was first introduced with lay majorities on the court and council but a senate made up solely of academic members. When Birmingham, the first institution to be granted a charter as a non-collegiate, unitary, university in England was founded in 1900, it was provided with a similar governance machinery but with the academic membership of the council amounting to a quarter (Ives, Drummond and Schwarz 2000). This latter degree of representation was in fact only achieved after substantial pressure from the professoriate and represented a more 'liberal' position than had been the case in Mason College, Birmingham's predecessor institution, where academic representation on the governing body was much lower and where the governing body had decisively overruled the academic board's wish to federate the College with the Victoria University based in Manchester.

The constitution of the civic universities which followed Birmingham set the pattern for what was to become the dominant governance model both for UK and for Commonwealth universities for most of the century. However, as Moodie and Eustace show, the period saw a steady shift of governance control away from courts and councils to representative academic bodies. Even in the 1900 charter and statutes Birmingham's council had the power 'to review and control or disallow any act of the Senate and give directions to be obeyed by the Senate' (quoted in Moodie and Eustace *ibid* a). While in the nineteenth century 'the internal powers of court and council were virtually unqualified' (Moodie and Eustace *ibid* b), the twentieth century saw their increasing qualification. Durham's new charter and statutes in 1937 were the first to declare the senate 'supreme' in academic matters, a formula that is common in charters and statutes of the 1960s' vintage. As late as 1936 the University Grants Committee was so concerned at the dominance of University College, Nottingham's council and the lack of academic representation on it that it withheld a recurrent grant increase until a revised constitution offered the senate five seats (Shinn 1986). Increasingly, statutes recognized the *de facto* partnership of councils and senates in internal self-government, accorded senates rights of consultation over statute amendments, academic appointments, the allocation of resources and, in some universities, policy towards site development. This, Moodie and Eustace concluded, represented 'a substantial move towards internal academic self government in all major areas of decision-making' (Moodie and Eustace *ibid* c).

In 1963 the Privy Council issued a model charter to guide the many new universities in the post-Robbins period that were seeking charters and statutes and this gave senates increased rights to initiate

and be consulted in major policy matters including rights of initiative in making appointments (Moodie and Eustace *ibid*). A typical
set of charter and statutes from this period, which may be taken as a
modernized version of the original civic university model, provided
for a carefully weighted distribution of powers. At the apex was a
court; this was shorn of the overall governing powers which had
been provided in the original civic universities in recognition of their
role in bringing the universities into being. In the first generation of
civic universities the powers had included the right to give final
approval for recommendations to the Privy Council for changes in
statutes, and it was rightly argued in the Dearing Report (NCIHE
1997) that this fettered the governing powers of the councils; they
were only withdrawn in some universities in the late 1990s. The
1960s' court retained only the power to appoint a chancellor and to
receive an annual report on the work of the university. The second
tier was provided by a council, made up broadly of two-thirds lay and
one-third academic members; student membership was generally not
conceded until the early 1970s. The council's powers were typically
defined in the charter as follows:

> There shall be a Council of the University ... which subject to
> the provisions of this Charter and of the Statutes, shall be the
> executive governing body of the University and shall have cus-
> tody and use of the Common Seal and shall be responsible for
> the management and administration of the revenue and prop-
> erty of the University and, subject to the powers of the Senate ...
> shall have general control over the conduct of the affairs of the
> University and shall have all such other powers and duties as
> may be conferred upon it by the Statutes.
> (University of Warwick 1998–99 a)

A senate provided a third tier:

> There shall be a Senate of the University ... which shall, subject
> to the powers of the Council ..., be responsible for the academic
> work of the University, both in teaching and in research, and for
> the regulation and superintendence of the education and dis-
> cipline of the students of the University.
> (University of Warwick *ibid* b)

However, the senate's position was strengthened by the wording of
the statutes which stated it to be:

> the supreme academic authority of the University and ... subject
> to the powers reserved to the Council by these statutes [able] to

take such measures and act in such a manner as shall appear to it best calculated to promote the academic work of the University...

(University of Warwick *ibid* c)

The respective detailed powers of council and senate were further set out in interlocking statutes which specified where a senate had powers that were advisory or recommendatory to council on particular issues or where council should take account of the views of the senate.

It would not be overstating the case to say that just as councils took over the operational governing powers of university courts in the early twentieth century, because courts were too big and met too infrequently and because university business was becoming too technical for them to be effective, so in the later twentieth century, and particularly in the post-war era, senates tended to take over the effective running of the universities from councils leaving the latter the formal powers of governance in legal and financial matters. There were three very potent reasons for this change: the first was that when, post-1945, the University Grants Committee (UGC) took over the funding of around 90 per cent of university expenditure the UGC's approach to funding, as might have been expected from a body whose membership was primarily academic, was largely aligned to academic interests and its operational rules and management style were aimed at the academic community; councils had to have UGC funding mechanisms explained to them by senates. Capital funding became mostly a UGC responsibility rather than, as had been the case between the two World Wars, of reliance on public appeals and external donors where lay members' links with the community could play an important part. The second was that the period saw a professionalization of the running of public services, whether in the new National Health Service or in the education service. In universities, professors who were playing notable roles in public affairs were much less willing to entrust their institutions to decision-making by councils made up of local worthies without their own close participation. As time went on professors found themselves under similar pressures as heads of departments or as members of senates from non-professors and, ultimately, from students who also wanted a share of decision-making.

Finally, this was a period of expansion. Contemporary documents record bitter complaints about financial stringency but in an expanding system where the UGC was anxious, with Treasury support, to maintain the unit of resource, arguments over funding with the UGC were more about the rate of growth, delays in funding the capital programme to keep up with the student numbers or the prospects for the next Quinquennial funding round, rather than about real reductions in budget. Councils and finance committees may have found themselves deferring new projects or juggling options but until the late 1970s the universities did not have to face hard strategic choices arising from year-on-year budget reductions. In the 1960s and 70s the real arguments in universities were largely about the determination of academic priorities and these, it was recognized, were best left to the academic community to resolve in the senate.

These conditions were to change sharply with the arrival of the Thatcher Government in 1979 and the UGC found itself not only rationalizing subject provision within universities, beginning with Russian Studies in 1979, but then in 1981 making selective decisions between institutions in the distribution of budget reductions system wide. The Government's decision not to continue to include overseas students in recurrent grant calculations but to encourage universities to charge full-cost fees represented an opening up of an overseas student market that had not existed before. An early retirement fund, administered by the UGC, gave universities for the first time the ability to declare consenting academic and non-academic members of staff redundant to reduce salary costs. On the whole most universities coped well and responsibly with the unwelcome decision-making required and the only large study of the management of the 1981 cuts, funded by the Department of Education and Science (DES) demonstrates this concluding that 'the implementation of the cuts of 1981 did not have universally negative impacts on cohesiveness, vitality, sense of purpose and mission, nor on morale' (Sizer 1987 a). Nevertheless, the welter of public criticism of the cuts emanating from the universities prompted the establishment in 1984 of a series of efficiency studies of university management, nominally organized by the Committee of Vice-Chancellors and Principals (CVCP) but in practice driven and funded by the DES in association with the Cabinet Office Efficiency Unit. These studies were coordinated by a Steering Committee under the chairmanship of Sir Alex (later Lord) Jarratt. The Committee's final report raised important and ultimately influential issues over the relationship between councils and senates in a period where some future financial turbulence was to be expected. Having described the essential features of the bicameral system it found that:

> the precise relationship between Council and Senate varies considerably. In some cases Council has ultimate powers in all matters; in others Council has to seek Senate's advice; in some,

especially where actions affect academic questions Council can only act with a recommendation from the Senate. Whatever the formal situation, intervention by Council in purely academic affairs is a rare event and in recent years Councils have accepted that they should seek Senates' views on many issues. This traditional division of effective roles is one not familiar to senior managers in industry or even in local authorities and civil service departments. The special powers vested in the Senate stem from the inherent nature of teaching and research and enable it to protect academic freedom. However, in times of financial constraint the potential for friction between Council and Senate is increased; and the changing circumstances of universities since 1981 are now leading to a questioning of the working relationship which prevailed throughout the period of expansion.

(CVCP 1985a)

The Report concluded that:

the relative decline in the exercising of influence by Councils has increased the potential for Senates to resist change and to exercise natural conservatism. Vice-Chancellors and university administrators have, in the past, been trained to believe that harmony between the two bodies should have a very high priority in a university. It may well be that a degree of tension between them is necessary in the circumstances now facing universities, and can be creative and beneficial in the long term. That can only happen if Councils assert themselves.

(CVCP *ibid* b)

The practical force, and the sentiments, lying behind this statement were to some extent ameliorated by the recommendation, generally attributed to Dr Geoffrey Lockwood, the only registrar member of the Committee, that universities should form joint council and senate planning and resource committees to integrate academic, financial and physical planning and to provide 'an effective bridge between the legitimate and different roles of Council and Senate' (CVCP *ibid* c). Nevertheless, the recommendation that senates' essential role should be to coordinate and endorse detailed academic work carried out in faculties and departments and be merely 'the main forum for generating an academic view and giving advice on broad issues to Council' (CVCP *ibid* d) represented a considerable reduction in the role that many senates had actually played (and in many pre-1992 universities continue to play) in the resolution of, for example, resource allocation decisions involving complex academic restructuring.

The Jarratt Report's recommendation that the balance of councils' and senates' roles should be readjusted in the light of the new circumstances led to a substantial shift in thinking in Whitehall and amongst Conservative Party politicians. From 1984 onwards legislation, for example on freedom of speech, laid responsibilities not on the universities corporately or on their senates but on their councils. The mechanism of the Financial Memorandum, which was introduced after 1988 to create a contract between a Funding Council and an HEI for the education of set numbers of students against a financial allocation, made the governing body, not the institution, accountable for delivery. Implicitly, the role of governing bodies continued to be enhanced to the exclusion of senates: the Dearing Report saw governing bodies as responsible for an 'institution's strategic direction, reputation, financial well being, the well being of staff and students, and, in association with Senate or Academic Board, for establishing and maintaining high standards of academic conduct and probity' (NCIHE 1997a) and stated that 'The performance of an institution', which might have been thought to be a reflection of the academic work of the university, 'was at the centre of a governing body's responsibilities' (NCIHE *ibid* b). The Lambert Report saw the governing body as having an important role in relations with industry and commerce. The fact that from 1994 a Committee of University Chairmen (CUC) produced authoritative *Guides on Governance* in higher education emphasized the perception that, conceptually, governance and governing bodies were somehow interchangeable. Thirty years after the publication of *Power and Authority in British Universities* the concluding sentence of Moodie and Eustace's book

> The supreme authority, providing that it is exercised in ways responsive to others, must therefore continue to rest with the academics for no one else seems sufficiently qualified to regulate the public affairs of scholars
>
> (Moodie and Eustace *ibid* d)

no longer reflected the way university governance was perceived. The civic university model, even though its bicameral structure was protected by charters and statutes, was interpreted by external authorities as operating much more like the way it did at the beginning of the twentieth century when governing bodies exercised a dominant role.

The Higher Education Corporation model ▮

An important reason for this was the arrival of a fourth model, the Higher Education Corporation (HEC). HECs were first created by legislation in 1988 (the Education Reform Act) when polytechnics and other higher education institutions, were transferred from local authority control to be independent corporations. In 1992 the Further and Higher Education Act designated the polytechnics and Scottish central institutions as universities. The HEC model was significantly different to the civic university model (and of course to the Oxbridge and ancient Scottish university models) in several important ways. First, the corporate body was no longer co-terminus with the institution itself but was vested in the governing body alone. Thus, whereas in the civic university model the corporate body comprised the whole university and its members included *inter alia* the staff, students and graduates of the university on behalf of whom it was governed by courts, councils and senates, each with prescribed memberships and powers, in the HECs the governing body itself was the corporation. Second, bicameralism as a legal concept was virtually dispensed with and a unicameral structure adopted. The polytechnics had weak academic boards (Jones and Kiloh 1987, Pratt 1997), and the Report of the Good Management Practice Group (NAB 1987) which paralleled the Jarratt Report for what was then the public sector of higher education did not even refer to them in its recommendations. Governing bodies were given the responsibility for the determination of the educational character and mission of their institutions and academic boards were restricted to advising their governing bodies on academic developments and resource needs, not direct, but through the vice-chancellor, or advising on matters which had been referred to them by governing bodies. Governing bodies were restricted to 24 members with only two, or in some institutions, three academic members.

Thus a typical post–1992 university governing body was responsible *inter alia* for:

(b) the determination of the educational character and mission of the University and the overseeing of its activities;

(c) the effective and efficient use of resources, the solvency of the University and the safeguarding of its assets;

(d) the consideration and, if thought fit, approval of the annual estimates of income and expenditure prepared by the Rector (Vice-Chancellor).

(University of Westminster 2005a)

And for all matters to do with the appointment and employment conditions of staff. The academic board, on the other hand, while responsible for academic activities including 'academic standards' was, subject to the 'overall responsibilities' of the governing body and the responsibilities of the vice-chancellor for these matters, and its formal involvement in policy was restricted as follows:

(b) consideration of the development of the activities of the University and the resources needed to support them, and the provision of advice thereon to the Rector and to the Court of Governors;

(c) the provision of advice in such other matters as the Court of Governors or the Rector may refer to the Academic Council.
(University of Westminster *ibid* b).

These arrangements reflected in part the backgrounds of the institutions involved. Local authorities had played a dominant role on governing bodies before 1988 and the members appointed by government from industry, commerce and the professions who replaced them saw no reason to change the position especially as they had the task of governing institutions which, on transfer, lacked well-ordered financial management structures and appropriate physical resources, and had no inherited financial reserves. The new governors brought expertise to the institutions which was crucial to their survival in the early years, rather as the members of university councils did in the unstable financial conditions of the first part of the previous century. In the case of the polytechnics previously controlled by the Inner London Education Authority (such as the University of Westminster whose instruments and articles are quoted above) these institutions had already been accorded a company structure by the Authority to encourage their independence and the existing company board structure simply moved with them into HEC and university status. Knight raises the question as to why the process of translation to university status was handled differently to the former colleges of advanced technology in the early 1960s which adopted the 'civic university' constitution (Knight 2002) and one must assume that the answer lies more in the Government's political imperatives and the maturity of the polytechnics, most of which had been in existence for more than 20 years, but the decision to depart so radically from the civic university bicameral model also reflected the influence of the Jarratt Committee. Although conditions were different in the polytechnics – academic staff were more unionized than in the universities and more robust in some institutions in labour relations issues, and relations between staff, management and governing bodies were much more affected by employment issues – one must conclude that the radical break with the previous half-century represented a deliberate policy shift. Subsequent incorporations of the HEC approach into policy towards governance in higher education, as referred to above, suggests that in Government, at least, the HEC model is seen to have advantages over the civic university model.

The US university governance model

If the Jarratt Report offered a significant steer away from the pre-1992 civic university model the HEC model essentially drew its inspiration from the polytechnic (and further education college) constitutions as initially created when the polytechnics were formed under local education authority control. In fact had the DES chosen to look internationally for governance models it would have found in the US a dominant unicameral structure of governance that quite closely paralleled the provisions of the 1988 and 1992 Acts. The seventeenth-century American colonial colleges drew partly on a Swiss Calvinist governing structure typified in the Geneva Academy and partly on Scottish university governance in the financial controls exercised by the Scottish courts. (When in 1868 the trustees of Princeton, looking for new leadership, appointed a Scottish divine, James McCosh to the presidency of the University they were following a precedent set 100 years previously in similar circumstances of appointing another Scot, John Witherspoon (Hoeveler 1981).) Yale's founding statute of 1701, received from the Connecticut General Court, vested authority in 11 ministers designated as trustees, partners or undertakers. Karp and Duryea (1979) conclude that: 'By the mid- eighteenth century, the government of American colleges lay irreversibly with external groups of lay trustees holding the status of corporations.' This model of a board which chose a president and oversaw his/her management of college affairs was extended to the public state and land grant universities which developed in the nineteenth century.

However, from the earliest period, we see rights and responsibilities ceded to the academic community. Thus Jasper Adams, a former college president, in an address in 1837 entitled 'On the Relation subsisting between the Board of Trustees and Faculty of a University' stated that 'no college in America has permanently flourished, in which the Trustees have not been willing to concede to the faculty, the rank, dignity, honor and influence which belong essentially to their station' (quoted in Hofstadter 1955 a). Hofstadter comments that 'in pointing out that those who expected to found colleges of repute that would survive and flourish must expect to delegate large powers to their faculties or fail [Adams] was simply generalising the whole experience of American academic life' (Hofstadter *ibid* b). The issue is perhaps summarized in a statement by the incoming president of a college in 1873: 'Professors are sometimes spoken of as working for the college. They are the college' (quoted in Hofstadter *ibid* c). If we look at the governance arrangements of the great US public universities what we see is a formal structure of a governing board with unicameral powers and with a president serving 'at the pleasure of the board' (that is without tenure in the post) but, underneath, a complex academic committee structure (and sometimes a formal senate) exerting huge influence on what the board decides. More surprisingly the faculty in major private universities are even more influential. Ehrenberg, a former Vice-President of Cornell, writing about the finances of the major private research intensive universities comments: 'It is hard to think of any decision made by the university in which faculty members do not feel they have a legitimate interest' and describes how governing boards have come to share governance responsibilities, not just in educational matters, with their faculty (Ehrenberg 2002).

The role of vice-chancellor in governance ∎

Important adjuncts to any discussion about governance in UK universities and colleges is the role of the vice-chancellor and the responsibilities of the registrar or clerk to the governors. Historically, it is clear that the vice-chancellor's role was always operationally important even in Oxbridge where colleges had a high degree of legal and practical independence from the university. Thus it is recorded of David Williams, who became Vice-Chancellor of Oxford in 1856, on the memorial to him in Salisbury Cathedral that 'he commanded the respect of the whole academic body by his prudent and *conciliating* (author's emphasis) administration and by his undeviating conscientiousness in the discharge of his duty' (Memorial to David Williams DCL, Salisbury Cathedral). This reflects the vice-chancellor's position as *primus inter pares* and the fact that in the nineteenth century at both Oxford and Cambridge the vice-chancellor was almost the sole administrator in the centre of the university. The Robbins Report, a little more than a century later, pays tribute to the importance of the role of the vice-chancellor in general and adds: 'No other enterprise would impose on its chairman the variety and burden of work that a modern university requires of its vice-chancellor' citing the vice-chancellor's key role not only inside the university but externally in the Committee of Vice-Chancellors and Principals (CVCP), communications with the UGC, and in fund-raising (Robbins' use of the word 'chairman' reflects a contemporary view of the importance of the senate *vis à vis* that of the governing body). (Committee on Higher Education 1963). A distinction, which in practice does not seem to imply a difference, is that in Scotland (ancient foundation or more recent) the title of Principal is used. (The title of President adopted by the merged University of Manchester appears again to have no particular legal significance, though it may reflect an intended change in style; it should not be confused with the post of President at the merged London Metropolitan University which appears to have a more honorary and ambassadorial role.)

Moodie and Eustace state that pre-1948 charters described the vice-chancellor as simply the 'chief academic officer' and that after that date the words 'and administrative' were inserted in new applications to the Privy Council marking a break between pre-war and post-war perceptions of the role. But we should be sceptical of trying to establish clearly demarcated stages in the evolution of the post as Bargh *et al* attempt to do in describing five phases in the post-war period (Bargh, Bocock, Smith and Scott 2000). Vice-chancellors like Morris at Leeds, Aitkin at Birmingham, Mansfield Cooper at Manchester or Hetherington at Glasgow were academic 'bruisers' in the post-Jarratt chief executive tradition who were successful academic leaders who in the 1950s and early 1960s drove their institutions through growth in student numbers and building programmes in a way which left their academic colleagues breathless and often resentful. They were often succeeded by less controversial figures, more arbitrators than initiators, but in the meantime Fulton at Sussex, Butterworth at Warwick and Carter at Lancaster showed similar leadership in building up a new generation of universities. The precise constitutional definitions of the power of a vice-chancellor give little indication of the potency of the role. The standard wording in the charter of a pre-1992 civic university model states no more than that:

> The Vice-Chancellor shall have a general responsibility to the Council and the Senate for maintaining and promoting the efficiency and good order of the University.
>
> (University of Warwick *ibid* d)

But within that bland formula there could be many variations in style and effectiveness. The Jarratt Committee, working in the aftermath of the most severe financial crisis in post-war university history, conducted studies in six universities and found some cases where the vice-chancellor saw his role 'primarily as that of a chairman seeking consensus' (not unlike the vice-chancellor of Oxford memorialized in the nineteenth century) and in others 'quite clearly as providing leadership and exercising executive authority'. The Report recommended that a vice-chancellor should be recognized 'not only as an academic leader but also as chief executive of the university'. But the Committee was exercised by the fact that vice-chancellors did not have formal powers and that they had to rely on 'the influence which stems from leadership and persuasion' and suggested that it lay within the power of governing bodies 'to strengthen formally the executive role of the Vice-Chancellor' (CVCP *ibid* e). Sizer, reporting only two years after Jarratt's call for 'executive leadership' offered a cautionary note that executive leadership could activate the 'off switches' as well as the 'on switches', in other words that care needed to be exercised that leadership did not give way to a style which over-emphasized authority and control (Sizer *ibid* b). Dearing, 12 years later, went further than Jarratt in arguing that a governing body should not simply provide a framework of authority for its vice-chancellor but also hold him/her accountable for achieving clear objectives (NCIHE *ibid* b).

Jarratt's characterization of the vice-chancellor as chief executive and the need to write that into the legal structure bore fruit in the 1992 legislation for the HECs where the position was greatly strengthened particularly at the expense of academic boards. The vice-chancellor was formally designated 'chief executive' and made responsible for presenting proposals to the governing body 'concerning the educational character and mission of the university' and for 'the organisation, direction and management of the university and leadership of the staff' (University of Westminster *ibid* c). These provisions mark a significant difference between the governance structures of the pre- and post-1992 universities, albeit differences of personal style can blur the distinctions. Investigations by Bargh *et al* (Bargh, Bocock, Smith, Scott *ibid*) and by Deem (Deem 1998) do not suggest that the differences that might seem to be conferred by the constitutional distinctions are necessarily borne out in practice, although a trend line would imply that while the HECs have a much more strongly marked executive culture than would be the case in the pre-1992 universities, some pre-1992 universities have now also moved significantly in the HEC direction while remaining formally constrained by the distribution of powers and responsibilities laid down in their statutes. It may be significant that the CUC Guide published in 2000 says that: 'He/she is, in effect, the chief executive of the university' (CUC 2000), while its successor states boldly: 'The head of the institution is chief executive of the university' (CUC

2004). As we shall see (Chapter 6) the exercise of this role has not been without controversy in the modern university either in pre- or post-1992 institutions and an important aspect of the definition of the balance of powers within institutional status is to provide safeguards against the abuse of power, a problem which is referred to only too often in the corporate world (cf. the Robert Maxwell case which inspired the Cadbury Report). The CUC Governance Code of Practice lays on the governing body the responsibility to put in place arrangements for monitoring the vice-chancellor's performance (CUC 2004) although reference to the salary levels paid to vice-chancellors (cf. *Times Higher Education Supplement* 2006) does not suggest that this mechanism works any more effectively than in industry.

The role of the secretary in governance

A second key figure in governance arrangements is the holder of the post entitled registrar or secretary (or registrar and secretary) in the pre-1992 universities and more often secretary or clerk to the governing body in the HECs. This distinction marks a significant difference of approach. In pre-1992 universities a registrar would normally be statutorily secretary not solely of the university council but of the senate, the faculty boards and all committees of these bodies and in addition would have managerial responsibilities either as the unitary head of the institution's administration, or as one of two or three senior officers (including the directors of finance and estates) reporting to the vice-chancellor. The Registrar of Oxford, and writing as a registrar with unitary managerial responsibilities, described this role very effectively, dividing the responsibilities into three defined areas: the secretarial, the managerial and the advisory to the vice-chancellor and chair of the governing body. On the first he set out the role as being:

> the steward of the constitutional and business rules and procedures; the coordinator of the flow of business in terms both of timing and content; the recorder of discussions/decisions and the transmission of them through the hopefully minimalist committee structure; and as the provider of information and papers on items of business (including the picking up of external signals and changes) – with now an increased emphasis on the independent role of the clerk to the governing body's role in corporate governance matters. Nobody should underestimate this function.
>
> (Holmes 1998 a)

A distinctive feature of such a post is that the secretarial role embraces the whole governance structure of an institution not simply the governing body itself. The registrar may not personally 'service' a faculty board but will be as concerned about the proper conduct of business there as at the senate and council where he/she might expect to take a personal responsibility for the discharge of business. Such a position acts as a guarantee for the way the institution as a whole reaches corporate decisions. Another feature is that the secretary is also a manager of major services for which he/she is answerable to the vice-chancellor so that the role has some of the characteristics of the permanent secretary of a government department with responsibilities for departmental management bound up with constitutional and advisory responsibility to ministers. It remains an important protection for a registrar in the pre-1922 universities that the post is legislated for in an institution's statutes and carries tenure so that the holder can only be dismissed 'for good cause' that is if he/she is unable for health or other compelling reasons to carry out the duties of the post or has committed some serious offence. This can provide a valuable safeguard in conflict situations and has been an important support where probity issues have arisen.

Such posts very rarely exist in HECs, which have typically opted much more for a company secretary role. This has the effect of distancing governing body procedures from, say, the academic board's and reflects the more dominant role in institutional governance of the governing body in post-1992 HEIs. Although most clerks to governing bodies have some other responsibilities they rarely correspond to the weight of these carried by the registrar in the pre-1992 universities and their advisory role is more likely to be restricted to procedural and legal issues than to matters of policy. (Some posts for example combine clerking with institutional legal responsibilities.) Whereas Holmes describes the third area of pre-1992 registrars' functions as:

> the provision of advice, strategic, tactical and operational to senior management both as a member of the university's senior management team and as a confidential adviser to the vice-chancellor and/or chairman of governors.
>
> (Holmes *ibid* b)

the post-1992 clerk may have a more restricted role, especially when cut off from financial management issues and disconnected from the work of executive pro-vice-chancellors who have line responsibility for the management of discrete areas of the institution's business.

Both types of post, however, share a heightened responsibility for the role of secretary to the governing body as a result of the governance scandals of the 1990s (described in Chapter 6) where governing bodies and/or heads of institutions were seen to act in inappropriate ways. As the marketization of higher education increases the importance of the secretary's role is likely to be enhanced, if only because the range of decisions likely to be faced by governing bodies and vice-chancellors will widen. But issues surrounding the reviews of governing body effectiveness, the role of audit committees and the operation of remuneration committees have all raised the profile of 'governance business' within higher education. The role of the secretary to a governing body in assisting the proper conduct of business has inevitably grown with it to the extent that the CUC *Guide* devotes more space to describing the role of the secretary or clerk to the governing body than to that of the vice-chancellor as head of the institution. It is worth quoting the CUC *Guide* here in full because it confirms the complexity of the role and seeks to define its responsibilities when things go wrong. In particular, it highlights the dual responsibilities of the secretary to the governing body and its chair, and to the vice-chancellor, where conflict exists or where inappropriate behaviour has occurred or is in prospect, and how such dilemmas can be resolved in accordance with the principles of good governance:

The secretary or clerk has a key role in the operation and conduct of the governing body, and in ensuring that appropriate procedures are followed:

a. The secretary or clerk to the governing body should be appointed to that post by the governing body.

b. Normally the secretary combines this function with a senior administrative or managerial role within the institution. The institution and the secretary must exercise care in maintaining a separation of the two functions. Irrespective of any other duties that the secretary may have within the institution, when dealing with governing body business the secretary will act on the instructions of the governing body itself.

c. In carrying out his/her role as secretary to the governing body, the secretary should be solely responsible to the governing body and should therefore have a direct reporting link to the chair of the governing body for the conduct of governing body business (i.e. agendas, paper, minutes etc.).

d. The chair and members of the governing body should look

to the secretary for guidance about their responsibilities under the charter, statutes, articles, ordinances and regulations to which they are subject, including legislation and the requirements of the Funding Council, and on how these responsibilities should be discharged. It is the responsibility of the secretary to alert the governing body if he/she believes that any proposed action would exceed the governing body's powers or be contrary to legislation or to the Funding Council's Financial Memorandum. (Note: the head of the institution is formally responsible for alerting the governing body if any action or policy is incompatible with the terms of the Financial Memorandum but this cannot absolve the secretary from having this responsibility as well.)

e.   The secretary should be solely responsible for providing legal advice to or obtaining it for the governing body, and advising it on all matters or procedure.

f.   The secretary should advise the chair in respect of any matters where conflict, potential or real, may occur between the governing body and the chief executive.

g.   The secretary should ensure that all documentation provided for members of the governing body is concise and its content appropriate.

It is incumbent on the governing body to safeguard the secretary's ability to carry out these responsibilities. It is important that the secretary also both consults and keeps the head of the institution fully informed on any matter relating to governing body business (other than in relation to the remuneration committee's consideration of the head of institution's emoluments). It is good practice for the chair of the governing body, the head of the institution and the secretary to the governing body to work closely together within the legal framework provided by the charter, statutes or articles of government and the ordinances and regulations laid down by the institution and the Funding Council's Financial Memorandum. If this is not possible because of inappropriate conduct by one of the parties involved, it is the responsibility of the governing body to take appropriate action.

If there is a conflict of interest, actual or potential, on any matter between the secretary's administrative or managerial responsibilities within the institution and his/her responsibilities as a secretary to the governing body, it is the secretary's responsibility to draw it to the attention of the governing body. If the governing body believes that it has identified such a conflict of interest itself the chair should seek advice from the head of the institution, but must offer the secretary an opportunity to respond to any such question.

(CUC 2004 c)

This statement puts the secretary at the heart of the governance process in a way that would not have been conceivable prior to the events in the mid-1990s.

Deans and pro-vice-chancellors

Similar differences occur between the pre- and the post-1992 universities in respect to the officers within academic governance structures, although there has been some blurring as organizational change has proceeded. In the 1960s it was the common rule that in pre-1992 universities deans were elected for two or three year periods (apart from deans of medical schools) from within their own faculties. In the 1990s, with financial devolution to faculties occurring in many universities, the post of dean, which had previously been thought of as the representative of the faculty, often became a fixed-term full-time appointment with line management responsibilities to the vice-chancellor. While this is the norm in post-1992 universities it has now been adopted in some pre-1992 institutions. In some pre-1992 universities, where faculties have been merged to make larger academic units, super-deanships have been created, sometimes called provosts or even pro-vice-chancellors, posts which are publicly advertised and highly paid for their managerial skills and, where appointments carry with them clearly defined managerial targets, usually associated with success in the Research Assessment Exercise (RAE). At the same time there has been a tendency in some pre-1992 universities for pro-vice-chancellorships, previously part time posts doubling up chairing senate committees in the place of the vice-chancellor with normal academic duties, to become full-time appointments and, if not formally full time, to have become so onerous and time consuming that they become natural springboards to vice-chancellor posts. In only a very few pre-1992 universities have these posts, however, acquired line management responsibilities over central administrative functions, although where a dean or pro-vice-chancellor is the budget holder for a faculty, this often carries responsibility for administrative staff within the faculty.

In post-1992 universities it would, however, be normal for pro-vice-chancellors to hold full time managerial appointments, usually publicly advertised, and for the central administrative functions to be divided up between them with a director of finance and some-times the director of estates and directors of human resources themselves being accorded the title of pro-vice-chancellor in a line management structure reporting to the vice-chancellor. Such post holders will at the least be members of the senior management team. At the next level down deans will invariably be full-time appoint-ments again often appointed from outside the institution. Again, almost invariably, deans will be budget holders for their faculties with a priority remit to work within their budgets and avoid deficits. In this structure, heads of departments will have a reporting re-sponsibility to the dean, and not to the vice-chancellor as would be the case in most pre-1992 universities and will be dependent on the dean for resources against fulfilling student number targets. What we see here is a much greater investment in an institutional executive and in vertical line management through the institution. In gov-ernance terms this has the effect of emphasizing the role of the body to which the executive is responsible. While this is legislated for in the case of the HECs the position is less clear cut in the pre-1992 universities where the powers of the senate provide a second level of accountability.

Heads of departments

Becher and Kogan describe the department as the basic academic unit and state that this unit is particularly important in the determination of professional values and in the maintenance of particular areas of academic expertise (Becher and Kogan 1992); they do not discuss the question of departmental leadership, and how such appointments are made. Bolton, in an otherwise excellent book *Managing the Academic Unit*, is similarly silent (Bolton 2000) and we have to go back to Moodie and Eustace, writing of an earlier age of post-1992 uni-versities, to find a discussion about the position of departments in overall institutional governance structures. Again we see pressures for change both from external and internal sources. For example nowhere was the radical fire of 'democratization' more evident than in the objections, in the 1960s, to the principle of professors holding permanent headships of departments, and increasingly universities adopted either electoral procedures or processes whereby the vice-chancellor consulted the academic staff members of a department as a means of identifying a head to serve for three or five years. As a result non-professorial heads became more common. These issues had mostly been resolved in the pre-1992 universities when the Jarratt Report recommended, by analogy with line management procedures in the wider world, a reversion to earlier practice that heads of departments should be appointed by the governing body (CVCP *ibid*) which led to most universities devising mechanisms whereby the more participative approach by then adopted could be incorporated into a formal recommendation by the vice-chancellor to the governing body. In the post-1992 institutions, however, the appointment of permanent heads of departments was normal practice when the incorporation process took place in 1988 and in some it has been continued. Where it has been varied the move to term appointments has led, because of grading and salary implications, to the initiation of formal appointment processes where applications are invited and appointments are made by the executive.

In both pre- and post-1992 universities accountability pressures and the downward pressure of resource management has tended to distance the role of head of department, even in the most collegial of universities, from the rest of the academic staff. Departmental meetings, while important for achieving consensus on issues, are now more advisory to the head of department in whom formal powers are invested by the university itself. The head may delegate some of these powers to named colleagues, such as for admissions or for health and safety, but must retain ultimate personal responsibility. This can reduce the role of individual academics to that of mere foot soldiers and the loss of personal involvement, especially in large departments, can have a long-term impact in discouraging academics from seeking a wider role in university governance.

University governance and the changing environment ▉

As we have seen, the balance of university governance structures has changed over the last century and cannot be regarded as immutable. Even now there are extremes. An investigation into university governance structures for the 1997 Commission of Inquiry into the governance of Oxford (the North Committee) threw up the case of De Montfort University which was described as having:

> a compact top structure with a small Board of Governors working closely with a Chief Executive ... who really is the Chief Executive and has considerable delegated powers, the Chief Executive runs the institution with the Senior Executive including four Pro-Vice-Chancellors, two Associate Vice-Chancellors, the Director of Finance, the Academic Registrar and the Director of Personnel ... There is a matrix management structure...
>
> (Commission of Inquiry 1997 a)

At the other extreme the investigation found Cambridge of which it said:

> People at Cambridge see the University as a largely self govern-
> ing 'community of scholars' with relatively little outside lay
> advice – not a top down managed institution. The academics
> work very hard – but 'would be unlikely to have the same mo-
> tivation' under the regime of the latter type. 'The present system
> works well and it would be absurd to change it'. The problem is
> to keep this ethos while meeting the demands of the new world
> for which the University must be well organised.
>
> (Commission of Inquiry *ibid* b)

The report concluded that:

> I am increasingly convinced that no one really knows how
> Cambridge works – perhaps because there are few really clear
> rules and each part of the system develops more or less in-
> dependently of other parts.
>
> (Commission of Inquiry *ibid* c)

Subsequent events, such as the Capsa affair (Chapter 6), showed the correctness of this conclusion and the problems which resulted al-though in academic terms the University still occupied a pre-emi-nent place in the UK university system.

Middlehurst has described the operating environment for uni-versities as being 'volatile, complex and increasingly demanding at all levels of the institution' (Middlehurst 2004) and the evidence suggests that while the organizational cultures which derive from the differing constitutional structures may still point to very different organizational solutions the joint pressures of the RAE, size and a continuing pressure on resources have pushed both pre- and post-1992 institutions to some degree further down a more formally managed route. In itself this may be less significant than the fact that these managerial routes can derive their effectiveness more from the executive than from the deliberative bodies, from vice-chancellors and senior management teams and from governing bodies rather than from senates and certainly very rarely from academic boards. This has had the effect of changing the way university business is conducted even in the civic university model which in terms of its formal constitution has remained not much changed since the 1960s. An important consequence is that the individual member of staff is much less closely connected with the governance process than in the past. This loss of personal involvement, which in the

1960s and 1970s remained very strong, in the pre-1992 universities, may have a long-term impact on the interest of the academic community in playing the full part in university governance that the pre-1992 charters and statutes, at least, envisage.

3

UNIVERSITIES AND THE STATE

It is impossible to think about institutional governance without recognizing the dimension that is provided by the influence of the
state. It needs to be borne in mind that, unlike universities in continental Europe, the dominant role model institutions in UK higher
education, the universities and university colleges founded before
1945, were all established through private enterprise which owed
nothing, apart from occasional encouragement, to state support.
This has given UK HEIs, including the HECs founded in 1992, an
expectation and perception of intrinsic operational autonomy
which, even though like the 1960s' new universities, they may have
been largely funded by the state, is very different to the position to be
found in many other higher education systems. It is, however a
paradox that as universities' apparent dependence on state income
has decreased in the last decade so the direct involvement of the
state, and the sense of state direction has tended to increase. Partly
this is because of the new demands for accountability, both financial
and in respect to policy, and partly because financial stringency has
made every institution more responsive to the need to compete for
funding from the latest government initiative. Both explanations
have an impact on governance.

Accountability to Parliament

A change in approach to accountability was inevitable as the higher
education system expanded but it was brought to a head by the
Cardiff affair in 1987 (Shattock 1994). Previous to this, and from the
point when the UGC was transferred from the Treasury to the DES in

1964, the permanent secretary of the DES was the accounting officer
for the expenditure of government funds in the university system,
although operationally the chairman of the UGC had responsibility,
with his committee, for the allocation of these funds to legally autonomous universities. Although the decision to give the Comptroller and Auditor General access to university accounts in 1962
occasioned a great deal of argument about the implied loss of autonomy, in practice the impact had not been very great.

However, the situation was essentially untidy. The Croham Committee Review of the UGC, which was much influenced by the un-
folding Cardiff affair, reported in February 1987 that:

> By long standing convention, the UGC is closely involved in an
> enquiry by the Comptroller and Auditor General into uni-
> versities' expenditure, and the Permanent Secretary is accom-
> panied by the Chairman of the UGC in appearance before the
> Public Accounts Committee of the House of Commons. The
> present position is unsatisfactory, because the DES Permanent
> Secretary is required to account for expenditure over which he
> has in general no effective control and about which the in-
> formation available to him may be limited by the conventions
> associated with the UGC's freedom of action.
>
> (Croham Report 1987)

In 1984–85 the UGC began to be concerned about the financial
management of University College, Cardiff, a constituent college of
the University of Wales, but a fully independent institution as far as
the UGC's grant list was concerned. By the summer of 1986 the
chairman of the UGC was sufficiently concerned to have reported
the matter to the permanent secretary since as chairman he had no
formal power to intervene where the head of an institution and its
governing body were unwilling to accept advice. No such question as
to the financial autonomy of an institution *vis à vis* accountability for
government funding had ever arisen before. The permanent secretary, formally advised by the chairman of the UGC, asked for an
independent set of accounts to be drawn up and, on the basis of the
figures provided by Price Waterhouse, the UGC suspended Cardiff's
recurrent grant until it had accepted advice as to how to clear its
deficit and put its affairs back into order. Even sending the Principal
on 'garden leave', suspending the bursar and advertising for a new
registrar was insufficient to achieve this and a takeover by the much
better managed University of Wales Institute of Science and Technology had to be put in place to rescue the institution, now Cardiff
University. The shock waves of the procedural dilemmas for the

fiduciary position of universities bore fruit immediately in the issue of new audit regulations, and hearings by the Public Accounts Committee. These hearings effectively exonerated the DES but severely blamed the UGC in words that effectively spelt out a redefined relationship between universities and the state:

> Respect for the independence of the universities is important but this does not mean that the UGC should have abjured sufficient control to be able to assure themselves of competent financial performance by universities.
>
> (Committee of Public Accounts 1990a)

By this time the 1988 Act had swept away the UGC and replaced it with a Universities Funding Council (and a Polytechnics and Colleges Funding Council) where in both cases the chief executive officer of the Council became the accounting officer for the system. Four years later the devolution of responsibility for higher education to the Scottish Parliament and the Welsh Assembly led to the creation of three unitary funding councils where this accountability model was repeated. In his evidence to the Public Accounts Committee in its hearings on the Cardiff affair the Permanent Secretary of the DES made it clear that:

> A principal objective in making this change [from the UGC to UFC] is to re-order and clarify responsibilities for propriety and value for money in relation to the public funding made available to universities.
>
> (Committee of Public Accounts 1990b)

Accountability is now delivered primarily through three instruments all of which have significant impacts on governance arrangements. These are the Financial Memorandum, HEIs' accounts and the HEIs' audit committees.

The Financial Memorandum

The operation of the Memorandum is controlled by an accountability framework which depends on three parties. The first is the chief executive of the funding council who is:

> responsible and accountable to Parliament [in the case of the Higher Education Funding Council for England (HEFCE) for ensuring that funds received from the Secretary of State [in the

case of England] are used for the purposes for which they were given and in ways that comply with the conditions attached to them.

(HEFCE 2000b)

The second is the institutional governing body which 'is ultimately responsible for the stewardship of those funds' and the third is a 'principal officer of the institution', normally the vice-chancellor, designated by the governing body who 'will need to satisfy the governing body that the conditions of this memorandum are complied with' (HEFCE 2000 c) and 'who is required to inform the governing body if any of its policies or proposed actions conflict with the Memorandum' and, if the governing body declines to fall in line, to report the matter to the chief executive of the funding council. If such a case has occurred it has not been reported, but the designation of the principal officer, while it may appear a formality, has in at least one significant case not been so. The issue arose in the merger of London Guildhall University with the University of North London where the vice-chancellor of the latter institution was designated the 'principal officer' and chief executive, but the vice-chancellor of the former remained vice-chancellor of the merged institution. There was obvious difficulty in assimilating two vice-chancellors in a merger situation but the designation of 'principal officer' gave a clear indication of who ultimately was responsible for the financial management of the merger.

The Financial Memorandum, while it does not fundamentally change a governing body's responsibilities from those laid down in statutes or articles, nevertheless has the effect of considerably sharpening them if you are a member. Thus the governing body 'must ensure that [the institution] has a sound system of internal financial management control' a responsibility which in at least one case has encouraged a governing body to overrule its officers, in the light of a particular incident, to spend funds reserved for academic expenditure on a new financial accounting system. The governing body is ultimately responsible for solvency (a point that arose particularly from Cardiff) and for ensuring that deficits do not exceed levels defined in the Memorandum. The Memorandum also lays down levels of borrowing that cannot be exceeded without funding council consent and requires the governing body to take 'an informed decision' before agreeing to any long term financial commitment (HEFCE 2000 a). (In at least one case the governing body, however, fully advised by external professional advice, committed themselves to a bond issue which was to provoke a cash crisis and a scheduling of funding council payments to overcome it along with other painful measures –

see Chapter 6.) Written consent must be obtained from the funding council when negative cash flows reach a certain level. These conditions are not in themselves onerous but when taken together with the requirement that the governing body formally approves strategic plans, financial forecasts, estates strategies and human management resource strategies, all demanded by the funding council, they impose significant procedural and other responsibilities on the secretaries to governing bodies to ensure that these responsibilities can be demonstrated to have been met and a considerable burden of alertness on the members themselves. Compliance with these procedural aspects of governing body business can impose a considerable weight of paper about issues which fundamentally have been decided elsewhere in the governance structure and can distract from discussion of live and more immediate issues of policy.

University accounts and governance effectiveness ▪

Historically, universities produced their own accounts in their own way but in the wake of the 1981 cuts the UGC invited the CVCP to undertake a review of university accounting practice to bring university accounts into a better state of comparability and guidance was issued by the CVCP in 1985. However, the need to gain acceptance from the Accounting Standards Committee as a Statement of Recommended Accounting Practice (SORP) drove further change together with the increasing need for the UGC/funding councils to comply with toughening Government accounting standards. Not only must accounts be drawn up in a standard format but an institution must submit them to the funding council by the end of December after the conclusion of the accounting year. Perhaps the most significant change from a governance point of view is the requirement that the accounts should contain a statement of corporate governance. Behind this lies a philosophy drawn from the private sector and based on the Combined Code on Corporate Governance issued by the Financial Reporting Council.

While this is discussed further in Chapter 4 it is necessary here to outline the approach which the funding council has adopted. The HEFCE Audit Code defines corporate governance, by which it means governance at the governing body level, as:

> the means by which strategy is set and monitored, managers are held to account, risks are managed, stewardship responsibilities are discharged and viability is ensured.
>
> (HEFCE 2004 a)

and concludes that:

> If corporate governance is effective, an organisation can flourish and, in this context, external stakeholders can rely on that organisation ... It follows that if institutions can demonstrate that their corporate governance is effective then we can derive confidence and adjust the level of audit and monitoring accordingly.
>
> (HEFCE *ibid* b)

It goes on to indicate how an institution demonstrates effectiveness:

- by publishing reports of corporate governance reviews;
- by publishing a statement of internal control which describes an 'effective system of risk management, control and governance' which is in itself a 'powerful statement of corporate governance if it confirms that all key risks have been identified and managed';
- by publishing a statement of corporate governance in the accounts which should indicate where governance arrangements differ significantly from guidance issued by the CUC;
- by arranging for audit assurance including on the statement of internal control;
- by paying attention to the advice of internal and external auditors.
  (HEFCE *ibid* e).

There is something of a mediaeval theological pathology about this respect for self-reporting mechanisms designed to demonstrate corporate governance effectiveness, and the end result is to place governance structures and processes at the heart of a series of accountability firewalls designed to protect the public purse. Financial propriety and governance are linked through the Financial Memorandum and the Audit Code of Practice in a way that would not have been conceivable in the past and the formal demands placed on governing bodies have, in consequence, been multiplied.

The audit committee

A prime instrument for the protection of state funds is the governing body's audit committee, an element of governance more or less unknown in the university world until the late 1980s. Audit committees are tightly controlled in their responsibilities by a Code of Practice which offers model terms of reference, prescriptions on membership, on frequency of meetings and on operational details, and which contains requirements in respect to the independence of the committee's secretary. In an echo of Jarratt's recommendation on the relationship between councils and senates it suggests that the committee needs the independence 'to challenge the finance committee' (HEFCE 2004 d). The audit committee must produce an annual report which, having been considered by the governing body, must be sent to a funding council's head of assurance and audit. The key arm of the committee is the internal audit service, whose audit plans must be approved both by the committee and by the governing body and whose annual report must be submitted to the committee, the governing body and also to the funding council head of assurance and audit, as must the report of the external auditor. Both internal and external auditors have the right to address a governing body if their appointments are terminated. All such arrangements are of course monitored by the funding councils' own assurance and audit team which carries out regular institutional audits and which not only reports to the funding council audit committee on institutional compliance but may, in the case of an institution designated as being at risk, advise the funding council to impose a representative as an observer at governing body or audit committee meetings as a condition of grant. In addition, universities are subject to visits and reports by the funding councils' own auditors who may inquire into a wide range of issues and by the National Audit Office (NAO) which issues reports on various aspects of university accountability and on the funding councils' own audit functions as well as triggering hearings by the Public Accounts Committee.

Regrettably, events in higher and in further education in the 1980s and 1990s may be said to justify this concentration on the responsibilities of audit committees and on the funding councils' need for access to reports by internal auditors, audit committees and external auditors, but the effect at the institutional level is often seen as being one of micro management and interference. For those working on the front line, as it were, of an institution's relations with the funding councils and concerned with governance issues these measures can seem like an increasing encroachment on institutional autonomy, not, it may be said, that any individual step can be regarded as overstepping the legitimate interests of the state but that the totality of them represents a degree of control, oversight and potential for intervention which undermines the sense of institutional self-determination.

Moreover, it engenders two other characteristics which strike at the heart of effective governance. The first is the tendency to present what the state appears to want to see. At the level of individual strategy documents, it is clear that institutions often prefer to submit strategic plans which mirror funding council objectives rather than what in their own circumstances they will actually do. This is less true with respect to Scotland or Wales where the size of the higher education sectors makes institutional dissimulation much more easy to detect. But it is said that only a minority of institutions in England submit financial plans to which they are strategically committed. At the level of audit, the profusion of reports that must be submitted negate careful scrutiny and, in at least one case, an internal auditor's report which, in effect, qualified the institution's accounts drew no response from the funding councils' audit team at all (Shattock 2001). But the second characteristic, which is paralleled in the private sector (see Chapter 4) is that members of governing bodies are not in sympathy with the additional demands being placed upon them by the need for compliance at the detailed level required. Thus the comprehensiveness of the audit controls imposed by the Code can have the effect, if observed to the letter, of weakening their commitment rather than engaging it with a consequence that more is left to institutional officers to deal with thus contradicting the very purpose for which the mechanisms were designed. Audit committees become more difficult to find members for and the members, because the demands it places on their time are so great, are less likely to be engaged on a day-to-day basis professionally with business operations whether in the public or private sectors. Audit committees have not been notable for standing up to finance committees or vice-chancellors.

Universities' strategies and the state

One of the key tenets of modern thinking about the role of the governing body is in relation to institutional strategy. The Dearing Report refers to institutions requiring 'excellent governance [by which it meant the governing body] to steer the institution towards its strategic direction' (NCIHE 1997c) and the CUC Code, refers to the effective governing body 'determining its [institution's] future direction' (CUC 2004). Governing bodies are required to indicate that they have approved the institutional strategic plans submitted to funding councils. What is striking, however, is how much of an institution's strategy is effectively determined by the state or by its agents the funding councils. Thus at an important strategic level an institution's positioning within the higher education system is determined in great part by the RAE. All the evidence suggests that this is strongly determinist in that universities at the top of the RAE league tables stay there, their position reinforced by the funding it guarantees, and those at the bottom, the post-1992 institutions, were destined to be there by the circumstances of their much less research-active past. The major state investment in research, both capital and recurrent, is entirely academically led and the bidding is determined on academic grounds or is based by the funding council on past academic achievement so that governing bodies are only minimally involved. Whatever their ambitions for the institution, financial circumstances make it impossible for a governing body realistically to determine that its institution should significantly change its status to be research intensive if it is not so already or resist the downward pressure imposed on aspirant institutions by the national policy to concentrate research funding in fewer institutions. Funding for teaching is strictly formulaic and any strategic flexibility that might be available is negated by the Government's cap on student number expansion except in selected areas. Few governing bodies, even if offered the opportunity by their executive, see fit to alter internal funding priorities reflected in the funding formulae.

The dominance of state-formulated policies, often supported by separate funding streams in research, access, quality, economic competitiveness and regionality, can reduce institutional decision-making on strategy and mission to relatively low-level considerations of the staging of a building programme or how to balance the accounts. When the Secretary of State can send 41 separate instructions to the English Funding Council (DfES 2003) on the day of the publication of the White Paper *The Future of Higher Education* (DfES 2003) the relative position of governing bodies or indeed institutions as a whole in determining real institutional strategies are marginal. Elsewhere I have argued that universities have a choice between 'derived autonomy' where the institution essentially follows funding council policies and transmits funding council funding formulae direct to subject areas or 'self-directed autonomy' where an institution consciously follows an individualistic self-determined strategy (Shattock 2003b). There is no evidence of a governing body, on its own, directing an institution down such a latter route; where institutions can be said to have done so it has come from a joint engagement of senates, governing bodies and the executive working closely together.

In the immediate post-War period Berdahl was able to portray a 'benign' relationship between universities and the state (Berdahl 1959). Since the 1990s it would be true to say that it has become much more derivative. The State has utilized its powers over finance to influence institutional behaviour, as might have been expected when the system itself had become so large and the state's commitment had grown to current levels. But the impact on institutional governance of this has been to inhibit freedom of action and to predetermine strategic decisions. Governing bodies, senates/academic boards and vice-chancellors in the first decade of the twenty-first century are probably working in a more strategically constrained climate than at any time in the last century. The combination of a formidable, and externally imposed, accountability regime and of a highly circumscribed strategic environment has meant that governance at all levels has tended to become less about initiative and new development and much more about process and compliance.

4

CORPORATE GOVERNANCE IN UNIVERSITIES

If the Jarratt Report exercised a decisive influence on the governance structure of the HECs in the 1980s when they were removed from local authority control, reforms in the corporate governance of business have played a similarly decisive role in influencing the development of governance in the whole of higher education in the 1990s and beyond. To understand how this has taken place it is first necessary to explore the nature of the changes in the corporate sector.

Reforms in corporate governance in public companies

These began with the Robert Maxwell scandal when it emerged that not only were the affairs of the various Maxwell companies hopelessly entangled in a way that was beyond boards dominated by Maxwell and his family to comprehend or control but that the pension provision for employees had been dissipated in the business of the companies. This prompted the establishment of the Cadbury Committee on the Financial Aspects of Corporate Governance by the Financial Reporting Council of the London Stock Exchange. The Cadbury Report, published in 1992, was a landmark document from which much of the modern regulation on corporate governance in the public as well as the private sector derives. Its central recommendation was that all companies listed on the Stock Exchange should comply with its proposed Code of Best Practice and that companies should record a statement of compliance, which should be reviewed by their auditors, in their company reports. The Code itself made important recommendations about the separation of chairmen and chief executives roles to avoid a single individual having 'unfettered powers of decision' (Cadbury *ibid*) and about the need to appoint non-executive directors 'of sufficient calibre and number to carry sufficient weight in the board's decisions' who 'should bring an independent judgment to bear on issues of strategy, performance, resources, including key appointments, and standards of conduct' (Cadbury *ibid*). The board should have audit, remuneration and nomination committees; non-executive board members should comprise the membership of the former and be in a majority on the latter two bodies. The board secretary should not be removed except by the board as a whole (Cadbury *ibid*). Much of this best practice was transferred into higher education.

Cadbury was followed by the Greenbury Report on the remuneration of chief executives and other directors (1995) after a series of 'fat cat' scandals over chief executives' emoluments, and by the Hampel Committee which was set up in 1995, again by the Financial Reporting Council, to review the implementations of the Cadbury and Greenbury findings. The Hampel Report endorsed the Cadbury recommendations but submitted a revised code to the Stock Exchange. It also offered some cautionary words: too often, it suggested, companies were treating the Cadbury and Greenbury codes 'as sets of prescriptive rules' (Hampel 1998 b). It went on to say that 'box ticking' took no account of diversity amongst companies and within companies over time, and could provide an easier option than a proper 'pursuit of corporate governance objectives' (Hampel *ibid* b). 'Good corporate governance', it concluded, 'is not just a matter of prescribing particular corporate structures and complying with a number of hard and fast rules. There is a need for broad principles. All concerned should then apply these flexibly and with common sense to the varying circumstances of individual companies' (Hampel *ibid* c).

Hampel added a compelling paragraph:

> Business prosperity cannot be commanded. People, teamwork, leadership, enterprise, experience and skills are what really produce prosperity. There is no single formula to weld these together, and it is dangerous to encourage the belief that rules and regulations about structure will deliver success.
>
> (Hampel *ibid* a)

Five years later, in the heightened atmosphere provoked by subsequent events, Hampel, reflecting on his report wrote:

> For me, corporate governance is becoming over-complicated and risks stultifying business. Rules will not prevent deliberate fraud

so we must ensure sensible balance ... Sadly, however, experience suggests that the box ticking my committee deplored has increased.

(Hampel 2003)

The point was emphasized again in a report entitled *Corporate Governance. Improving Competitiveness and Access to Capital and Global Markets* issued also in 1998 by an international group, which included Cadbury, which stated:

> The primary role for regulation is to shape a corporate governance environment, compatible with societal values, that allows competition and market forces to work so that corporations can succeed in generating long term economic gain. Specific governance structures or practices will not necessarily fit all companies at all times. Nor should it be taken for granted that a given design may suit the same company during different stages of its development. For dynamic enterprises operating in a rapidly changing world, corporate adaptability and flexibility – supported by an enabling regulatory framework – is a prerequisite for better corporate performance.

(OECD 1998)

This mood of resistance to prescriptive regulation was significantly disturbed by the Enron collapse in December 2001 in the US where billions of dollars of debt were hidden by complex and dubious accounting practices. In April 2002 Arthur Andersen, the firm which had audited Enron, and which was assailed by law suits, investigations and client defections arising from its failure to blow the whistle on its clients' accounting practices, closed its doors. This was followed by the collapse of WorldCom in June 2002 accused of false accounting and by the resignation of the chairman and chief executive of Tyco also in June, indicted for tax evasion after his board had awarded him (he had been given a $40 million package in 2001) a contract running through to 2008 and 800,000 Tyco shares with no performance requirements. One reason adduced by the Tyco remuneration committee was that he had been named by *Business Week* as one the 25 most outstanding managers of the year. These events caused almost unprecedented concern in the US, because of a fear of a general collapse in the market. The root cause of these corporate failures, according to the Chairman of the Federal Reserve Bank was 'the enlargement of stock market capitalisations in the latter part of the 1990s'. It was not that people were greedier than at other times but that there was 'an outsize increase in opportunities for avarice' (Greenspan 2002). Another explanation put forward by a member of the UK Financial Accounting Standards Board was that 'the focus of the entire financial community [has been] on short term earnings' exacerbated by the tendency in the US for the average tenure of a chief executive to be no more than four years (Foster 2002). Whatever the cause, the Chairman of the Federal Reserve Bank went on to say:

> Lawyers, internal and external auditors, corporate boards, Wall Street security analysts, rating agencies and large institutional holders of stock all failed for one reason or another to detect and blow the whistle on those who breached the level of trust essential to well functioning markets.
>
> (Greenspan *ibid*)

This concern over corporate governance failure led to the passage of the Sarbanes–Oxley legislation (named after Senator Sarbanes and Congressman Oxley) in 2002, which brought in wide reform of US corporate governance, including measures intended to prevent corporate fraud and increase supervision of the accounting industry. The measures imposed, however, create substantial bureaucracy – one section, Section 404 which requires companies to report on their internal controls, and auditors to pass judgement on managements' assessments of and on the actual effectiveness of the controls, is especially burdensome. General Electric claims to have spent $30 million and 250,000 hours of employers' time putting these controls into place (Roberts 2004) and has led companies to employ significant numbers of financial compliance officers. One bank, for example, has had to employ 14 legal 'chaperons' to police conversations between analysts and investment bankers talking on certain subjects (Wighton 2004). The legislation, which is administered by the US Securities and Exchange Commission (SEC) extends to any company with a given number of US shareholders so that at least 50 UK companies are also involved in satisfying the SECs onerous requirements. Three issues stand out: the first is the impact the legislation is having on the way companies hire staff, structure themselves and work with lawyers and accountants; the second is the additional cost created, not just on a company's own internal operations, but arising out of its relations with customers and suppliers where there is also a need to satisfy the legislation's requirements; thirdly companies are finding it difficult to recruit board members, particularly for audit committees (Sherman 2005).

It is argued in the UK that because of the way corporate governance reform was begun as long ago as 1992 with Cadbury, the UK position is less extreme than is required by the Sarbanes–Oxley legislation which was over-reactive to demands for immediate safeguards. However, the impact of US corporate governance failures on the UK was considerable and resulted in a report: *Audit Committees Combined Code Guidance* (The Smith Guidance) issued in January 2003. The same month saw the issue of the Higgs *Review of the Role and Effectiveness of Non-executive Directors* (Higgs 2003) commissioned not by the Stock Exchange but by the Treasury and the Department of Trade and Industry. This was, in effect, a complete review of Cadbury and Hampel with more definition and teeth, but with an even greater concentration on the corporate governance role of non-executive directors. The Higgs' recommendations, after lengthy consultation, were incorporated into a new *Combined Code on Corporate Governance*, which includes the Smith Guidance on audit committees and the Turnbull Guidance on internal controls issued under the authority of the Financial Reporting Council (2003).

The effect of the growth of regulation in corporate governance in the private sector from Cadbury onwards explains, in great part, the increase in accountability requirements described in Chapter 3. As each new report appeared in the private sector, by analogy it was applied, often with added bureaucratic rigour in higher education, and in the voluntary and public sectors in general. The well-publicized cases of governance failure in higher education described in Chapter 6 made their interventionist character impossible to resist. It should not be assumed, however, that the new requirements have been easily assimilated in the business world nor that they have not had effects which are echoed in higher education. Two years after the issue of the post-Higgs' Combined Code the *Financial Times* reported an analysis of corporate governance statements of the FTSE 100 companies by a powerful shareholder body that less than half were on track to comply (Tucker 2004b). Meanwhile, companies had come to rely increasingly on head hunters to identify potential non-executive directors and non-executive pay had gone up nearly 40 per cent with committee chairmen receiving additional payments, the highest pay being for chairs of audit committees (Tucker 2004a). Annual fees for non-executive directors had gone up by 21 per cent 'as a result of higher work loads prompted by the Higgs report' and the pool of high quality non-executives had shrunk as many had become 'choosier' about the posts they were prepared to take (Tucker 2005). One solution was for companies to look overseas for non-executives (Tricks 2005). A MORI poll of 105 chairs, chief executives and finance directors of FTSE 500 companies said that 70 per cent of respondents indicated a reluctance to take on the chairmanship of an audit committee because of the time and the legal and other risks

involved without the financial compensation and the surety of efficient legal protection if things went wrong. In March 2005 the *Financial Times* reported that 'Regulatory fatigue is close to becoming a
global phenomenon' (Plender 2005). These concerns represent serious crossover issues in higher education where the supply of lay
members of governing bodies to sit on audit committees, which
demand increasing amounts of their time, is as much under pressure
as in the corporate sector. Regulatory fatigue and the costs associated
with over-regulation, while serious problems in themselves, are
perhaps not so serious as the impact the new accountability regimes
can have in restructuring the conduct of university business. Increasingly, governance is seen as comprising a series of technical
issues which are handled by specialists. The secretary or clerk to a
governing body becomes a master of procedure rather than a guide
on how to deal with real issues and the procedures become so
complicated and bureaucratic that not only does the job often become separated, *de facto* and sometimes *de jure*, from the post of
registrar, but real business is often driven away from participative
committees to executive decision-making. There is a temptation to
regard the process of taking a decision as more important than the
substance and to devise or reinforce decision-making structures that
fit formal accountability processes rather than reflect managerial
realities. Recruitment to audit committees, as in the private sector, is
increasingly difficult and on the two occasions referred to in Chapter
6 where audit committees were involved in serious governance issues, the audit committees proved to be ineffective. Perhaps most
important the analogies with accountability in the corporate world
concentrate attention and the conduct of business at the governing
body level on process to the detriment of consultation, participation
and decision-making (technically recommendation-making) at lower
levels of governance where academics and others are involved.

The role of boards of directors ■

The main thrust of the Cadbury reforms was that the decisions and
actions of the internal executive directors were made subject to
controls by non-executive directors who were appointed from outside but who under company law had the same *de jure* responsibilities
for the well-being of the company as the executive directors. The
Higgs' reforms took this matter further with a codification of non-
executive directors' responsibilities.
   It is not difficult to see why, in the light of the scandals in the

university sector in the 1990s, it was natural that a Government that had so committed itself to the post-1992 governance model should have therefore seen an easy analogy between boards of governors and boards of directors (after all, the former London polytechnics all had corporate status), and therefore the relevance of the Cadbury reforms. The trouble was that the analogy is by no means as clear cut when the issues are closely examined. Some useful pointers can be obtained from a Department of Trade and Industry (DTI) report on a company collapse, TransTec PLC, largely attributable to a failure in corporate governance (Aldous and Kaye 2003). The circumstances of the case were that the managing director and the finance director had committed themselves to financial obligations which were not reported to the board or to the audit committee and which had not been formally queried by the company's auditors. The report followed a special investigation under section 432(2) of the Companies Act 1985, conducted by two Inspectors, Hugh Aldous FCA and Roger Kaye QC, and was principally authorized because of the political sensitivity of the past involvement of Geoffrey Robinson MP, the company's founder. The report suggested that a board of directors should:

(a) hire the best chief executive they can find;
(b) understand the business, probe and assess its performance and competitive position;
(c) with the chief executive, develop objectives and a strategy for the business and set goals and priorities both for the long term sustainability of the business and for its short and medium term profitability;
(d) with the chief executive, adopt and monitor a strategic planning process and review operating plans;
(e) monitor the performance of the chief executive and senior management, assess their competence and replace them if necessary;
(f) set the culture and ethos of the board and the consequent style and standard of governance of the group;
(g) satisfy themselves that there are processes that ensure the integrity and appropriateness of management information and internal controls;
(h) satisfy themselves that the board's responsibility for risk management and internal control is effectively discharged by the management system; and
(i) assess their own contribution to the business.

(Aldous and Kaye *ibid* a)

At first glance one could almost transpose this definition of a board's duties to those of the governing body of an HEC but the area where the analogy crucially breaks down is the composition of the board. Most public companies would expect to have a roughly equal number of executive directors and non-executive directors. In the post-1992 university model, however, the vice-chancellor is the only member who could be described as 'executive' since the two or three other staff members are normally elected by staff constituencies and, in practice, often have a trades union affiliation, and the student members by definition are not 'executive'.

It is impossible to imagine any UK public company operating on the basis of one executive director and some 20 or so non-executive directors, plus some staff and consumer representatives. The civic university model, on this basis, might be seen as rather closer to the corporate model because the pro-vice-chancellors, who could be deemed 'executive', would normally be members of the governing body, *ex officio*, and the one-third academic membership would be nominated by the senate which has executive authority in academic matters. Academic members would not see themselves as being in an executive role, however and would seem to represent in company terms an unknown category of an internal non-executive director.

A second important difference from a company board lies in the background of the non-executive members. On a company board the non-executive members, while important in their scrutiny roles on audit and remuneration committees, will be selected from outside the company for the experience they bring to the company's business. They need, as the DTI report says, to be able to 'understand the business, probe and assess its performance and competitive position'. If we accept that a university's core business is delivering teaching and research one might expect to see people experienced in this being brought onto the board. In practice, what universities look for are people who bring business or professional experience and high-level management experience in other fields to the governing body. This means that they are literally laymen when confronted with issues that arise out of the core business, especially in areas of academic strategy, which most governing bodies might be expected to comment on but not to originate. A governing body would not, therefore, be able to satisfy the requirements (b), (c) and (d) of the DTI report's statement of a company board's responsibilities. These functions might either be carried out by a Jarratt-style planning and resources committee reporting to the governing body and senate, containing key members of the academic community, or by what Clark (1998) called 'the strengthened steering core', a senior academic and administrative group chaired by the vice-chancellor.

Company boards are expected, as the DTI report makes clear, 'to stay ahead of events and direct the business of the company' in a way which governing bodies are not equipped to do, except by drawing heavily on the expertise of the vice-chancellor and his/her staff and senior members of the academic community. In a university world dominated by funding council financial formulae, Research Assessment Exercise scores, league tables, recruitment and retention targets and overseas markets and the complexities relating to research grants and contracts and commercial exploitation, governing bodies need to work closely in partnership with academic bodies if they are to ensure they are 'monitoring the underlying health of the business rather than just the latest financial returns' (Aldous and Kaye *ibid* b).

A third reason the analogy is inaccurate relates back to the balance of executive to non-executive board members. In the case of Trans-Tec the essential reason for the failure of the company was that financial obligations were incurred by decisions taken by the managing director and the finance director which were not reported to the board and were not drawn to the board's attention by the auditors:

> Rather than challenge management the non-executive directors chose to rely on the auditors for assurance. They did not appreciate that the auditors were, like them, unwilling to challenge management and unwilling also to express a robust opinion.
>
> (Aldous and Kaye *ibid* c)

In this case the reliance on non-executive directors, many of whom were very knowledgeable as to the industry the company was in, was found to be misplaced. Perhaps we should not be so surprised by this. The chairman of the Treasury Select Committee, John McFall MP, at a conference called to consider the implications for UK business of the collapse of Enron, is quoted as saying:

> I have been on boards where I have a non-executive role – I've always found it hard to understand what the executives are up to and to be up with their thinking. And when someone is at work five, six, seven days a week and is responsible for the strategic focus and direction of the company and someone flits in once a week, or once a month I doubt that person has a chance against a real professional.
>
> (McFall 2002)

If this is true of someone who fully understands the business how much more is it true of governing body members, meeting normally no more than four or five times a year, who, if they have not worked in universities themselves, cannot be fully cognisant of the core business? Indeed the only detailed piece of published research on how governing bodies actually function in handling operational questions (admittedly of a small sample of post-1992 HECs) concludes that they:

> could be said to be very efficient but passive bodies in that they deal with a large number of items at board meetings but mostly without discussion or debate. They could be said to be rather ineffective bodies, not appearing to have any major impact on the strategic plans and major governance matters of their institutions or overly involved with the monitoring of executive performance.
>
> (Bennett 2002)

This statement could be paralleled by the DTI report's of a description of the TransTec board:

> Our impression is that throughout the period in which we enquired, TransTec's board was relatively passive, and very much dominated by its chief executives. We do not get the impression of a board that spent very much time understanding the business, or that met key customers, debated strategic options, planned ahead or particularly directed the business. We get the impression that Mr. Robinson and then Mr. Carr (his successor), had views on strategy and an idea of what they wanted to do – Mr. Carr, for his part, saw that to be achievable largely by acquisitions. We think that the board very largely listened to those views and went along with them.
>
> (Aldous and Kaye *ibid* d)

Since Bennett's conclusion was reached on only a small sample of non-universities (though most have since achieved a university title) it would be unwise to generalize from it too extensively although it is paralleled by a similar study in the voluntary and public sectors where boards' strategic contributions were similarly slight (Cornforth 2003).

It is also paralleled by research in the US where Chait and his colleagues undertook two in-depth and extensive studies of governing boards (Chait, Holland and Taylor 1991, Chait, Holland and Taylor 1996a) supported by the American Council for Education and a variety of grant-giving bodies. They concluded that 'effective governance is a relatively rare and unnatural act' (Chait *et al* 1996 *ibid* a) largely because boards concentrated on the immediate rather than the long-term issues:

> As part time amateurs largely unfamiliar with the organisations' culture, trustees are not especially well equipped to oversee the work of full time professionals and to be the ultimate arbiters of a prudent course of action. Without specialised knowledge, trustees tend to dwell on the more familiar realms of operations, finance and investment, usually to the neglect of the institution's core business.
>
> (Chait *et al ibid* b)

Trustees, they found, were well-intentioned, high-powered people who were engaged in low-level activities, and they quote trustees on this, who either defer uncritically to management or 'try to force a familiar corporate model on non-profit institutions'. (Chait *et al* 1996 *ibid* c).

The overall point that, without very frequent meetings, which would be unwelcome to most members, it is difficult to see how governing bodies can build up the necessary expertise and involvement in strategic decision-making to exercise the functions of a well-run company board, does not depend upon Bennett's conclusion. And it is one reason why governing bodies, unlike company boards, conduct much of their business through a committee structure, for example in relation to finance, where members can meet more frequently and become more familiar with the business in hand and there is a wider spread of in-house expertise present to help them to do so and guide their decisions. However, what Bennett's research does perhaps highlight is one reason why, where serious instances of misgovernance have occurred, it has been the academic community which has more often blown the whistle than members of the governing bodies.

The wider issue is the fact that a university governing body cannot, on its own, fulfill the requirements of a company board because it needs the detailed involvement of senior representatives of the academic community in the governance of the institution for it to be effective. A strong senate/academic board, working jointly with the governing body in areas such as strategy and resource allocation, brings together the vital constituents of good governance in a university context. The strength of the civic university model is that it builds such a partnership into a bicameral legal framework of governance. In the post-1992 model the legal framework is unicameral and the partnership, if it exists, has to be built up in spite of both the clear demarcation of responsibilities between the governing body and the academic board and the tendency for the post-1992 constitution to encourage the build-up of a strong management cadre around the vice-chancellor, as a designated chief executive, to the exclusion of a close involvement of senior members of the teaching and research community. It is important to note that some institutions have overcome these inhibiting legal prescriptions to establish the partnership necessary for successful university governance.

Perhaps the most obvious incorporation of the company board analogy into university governance is the concept of a Code of Governance. We have seen above how the Cadbury Code of Best Practice led eventually to the Combined Code on Corporate Governance, which was substantially revised as a result of the Higgs Review. In 1994, after the Huddersfield and Portsmouth scandals had hit the media, the Committee of University Chairmen (CUC) offered advice to the university sector particularly dealing with governance issues that had surfaced in the two institutions. In 1995 the CUC published a formal *Guide*, which it revised in 1998, 2000 and 2004 (CUC 1995, 1998, 2000, 2004). A distinctive feature of the *Guides* was that they were issued by the CUC in conjunction with the CVCP/ Universities UK and the Association of Heads of University Administration (AHUA), the body representing registrars and secretaries and that they recognized the structural differences in governance between the pre-1992 and the post-1992 universities arising from their different legal identities. In adopting this approach the CUC was implicitly following the conclusion of the Nolan Committee on Standards in Public Life which had conducted an inquiry into university governance in the wake of the concerns (and which had commended the *Guide*) which had stated that:

> Many of the institutions have evolved systems of governance over many years and it would require evidence of substantial misconduct to justify sweeping changes. We received no such evidence.
>
> (Committee on Standards in Public Life 1996)

This was confirmation that there was no case for seeking to reform in any fundamental way the legal framework of university governance, although the Committee made a number of recommendations in regard to questions of practice. The idea of a Governance Code, modelled seemingly on the basis of the Combined Code, first surfaced in the Dearing Report. Dearing argued that institutions faced: 'a degree of change ... more profound than that experienced in the recent expansion' and that the task of governance was 'to steer the institution towards its strategic direction' (NCIHE 1997c). It did not think that the *Guide* addressed 'a number of important structural matters' and it suggested that the purposes of a Code would be:

- to ensure that institutions governing bodies can make their decisions in a way that is effective;
- to provide a basis for familiarity with the governance arrangements within institutions;
- to ensure there is appropriate membership of the ultimate decision-making bodies;
- to ensure that governing bodies can meet their obligations to their wider constituencies inside and outside the institution.

(NCIHE *ibid* d)

These objectives might seem to be bland and uncontroversial enough but a further section prescribed what it felt should be the components of the Code. These included the unambiguous identity of the governing body – essentially the question referred to above where some civic university courts retained governance powers which overrode those of councils – and a number of issues covered fully in the *Guide*. But they also included a call to reduce the size of pre-1992 university councils to a limit of 25 and a recommendation that governing bodies should review their own effectiveness and the effectiveness of their institutions at five-yearly intervals including such matters as the size of the governing body. So insistent was the Report on this issue that it recommended that the publication of effectiveness reviews should be a condition of public funding, as should the publication of an annual report commenting on compliance with the Code.

Fortunately, the Government was resistant to this degree of prescription and accepted arguments that these issues, including the question of the size of the governing body, should be left to voluntary action. The result was a widespread review, by the pre-1992 universities themselves, of the size of their governing bodies, and a reduction of membership to around 33 (CUC 2000b). But underlying the Dearing recommendations was a move to set up processes which would over time force the pre-1992 universities to adopt a post-1992 size of governing body and implicitly endow those governing bodies with the same kind of unicameral powers of direction that obtained in the post-1992 universities, which themselves were closely modelled on company boards. The Report paid formal tribute to the importance of institutional autonomy but its thrust was to pressure institutions to conform to a common governance model. The CUC, which represented the interest of universities, was, however, unwilling, at that time, to accept a Code both because, by analogy with the Combined Code it could be used to put pressure on institutions to comply with it and because it could be used as the thin end of a wedge to weaken the statutory framework laid down in charters and statutes conferred by the Privy Council. Although the essence of the *Guide* was its voluntary nature the HEFCE audit machinery came to use it very much as if it were a Code, and in their periodic visits to universities used the *Guide* as a check of good practice, requiring explanations where an institution deviated from a narrow mirroring of the *Guide's* recommended approach, thus copying the 'comply or explain' approach in the Combined Code. The idea of the Code was itself not dead, however, and was revived six years after Dearing in the Lambert Review of Business–University Collaboration (Lambert 2003).

The Review, established by the Treasury, to address industry–university links and relationships had added on to it, at a late stage, the issue of governance, it is said, because of concern about the failure of the Cambridge MIT link to deliver what the Treasury wanted. Hardly surprisingly, the Report offered an inexpert, and often inconsistent, commentary on governance issues. Its tone can be judged by a statement that:

> The older universities were, historically, run as communities of scholars. Their management and governance arrangements were participatory: senates and councils were large and conservative
>
> (Lambert *ibid* a)

This suggests that to be 'participatory' is somehow a governance weakness. It praises 'dynamic management in an environment where decisions cannot wait for the next committee meeting' (Lambert *ibid* b) a phrase which could describe the root cause of some of the cases of misgovernance quoted in Chapter 6 or indeed decision-making in Government, in the more rarified context of the Butler Report where 'the informality and circumscribed character' of the decision-making procedures reduced 'the scope for informed collective political judgement' (Butler 2004). In commending the post-1992 university constitutions where 'governance is the responsibility of a small 12–24 person, lay-dominated, independent governing body' (the company board model) the Report did not draw the obvious, counter-intuitive conclusion that in terms of business–university collaboration it was the universities with 'participatory' and apparently inefficient governance structures which had the innovative links and large research collaborations with business and where 'the innovative ideas that are being developed in scores of departments in dozens of British university campuses' (Lambert *ibid* c) were mostly present, rather than in universities that had 'lay-dominated, independent' governing bodies. The Report went on explicitly to make the analogy of the revision of the Combined Code following the Higgs Review as an argument for recommending that the CUC should develop a Code which should be voluntary but where 'all institutions should disclose in their annual report when their governance arrangements do not conform to the code and explain why their governance arrangements are more effective' (Lambert *ibid* d).

The Report offered its own version of a Code which, unsurprisingly, suggested that the maximum membership of a governing body should be 25 and that meetings should be held 'sufficiently regularly' and not less than once a quarter. Rather than five-yearly reviews of effectiveness it recommended they should be conducted at least every two or three years. Disappointingly, the CUC this time (2004) conceded a Governance Code of Practice which largely followed the Lambert template. It worded the question of membership rather differently regarding the figure 25 as 'a benchmark of good practice' (CUC 2004 *ibid* g) and reverted to five-yearly effectiveness reviews as recommended by Dearing. It also avoided the danger of a confusion of authority by including a firm statement that:

> a governing body shall ensure compliance with the statutes, ordinances and provisions regulating the institution and its framework of governance and, subject to these, it shall take all final decisions on matters of fundamental concern to the institution.
>
> (CUC *ibid* h)

This is a very much less formidable document than the Combined Code but it still adds nothing to the provisions of the *Guide*, a revised version of which (CUC 2004) the CUC published simultaneously.

The 2000 edition of the *Guide* opened with the words:

> Institutions of higher education are characterised by a distinctive ethos. Despite diverse backgrounds and traditions they are united in the common purpose of the provision of teaching and the pursuit of knowledge and research, including research which contributes to economic growth.
>
> (CUC 2000)

This statement encapsulates the sense that universities need to preserve their academic identity from too close an identification with private sector corporate governance which could too easily be used as a justification for imposing a structure that Cadbury defined as 'The system by which companies are directed and controlled' (Cadbury *ibid* c). This definition is too simple a formulation for the way universities are managed and ignores the evidence from the management of professional bodies like law firms and accountancy firms. These firms are traditionally, and for the most part remain, partnerships where each partner, not too unlike an academic in relation to teaching and research, has personal working autonomy because he/she has sole responsibility for dealing with a portfolio of clients. Historically, firms were quite small and corporate decisions about their management were taken at partners' meetings chaired by an elected managing partner supported by a senior partner. As firms have grown, and particularly after mergers, these partners meetings are no longer practicable (Clifford Chance is reported to have nearly 5000 lawyers in 19 countries), so that fundamental questions have had to be faced about leadership, management and governance. In many cases partnerships have voted to bring in managers from outside the profession to take charge, in collaboration with subsets of partners, and have voted to float the firm and thereby take on a full corporate structure. The point to note, however, is that professionals, whose reaction to corporate management is much like that of academics, have found it possible within the partnership framework to reach decisions about mergers, takeovers and restructuring without 'lay-dominated, independent' boards at all (Skapinker 2002). Clifford Chance with 650 partners and a turnover of over £1 billion, takes its most important decisions by postal ballot amongst its partners, perhaps balloting them ten times a year. Oxford and Cambridge colleges are self-governing in an almost exactly parallel way and have business decisions to take over property and investments that are at least as critical to their survival as the decision-making which occurs at partnership meetings. This is not to argue that the civic or even the HEC models are not valid for the governance of university institutions or that lay members do not make vital contributions but just to emphasize that the corporate model, while fashionable in current thinking, is not the only external model from which useful analogies can be drawn. The introduction of a Governance Code, even if with only a slender likeness to the Combined Code, is a step towards turning an analogy into something like a derivative. It is important that the easy analogy with the corporate model is resisted not least because the functions of a university are different from those of a company and demand a different style of governance and management if they are to be successful.

We should also be careful about assuming that bureaucratic remedies will resolve the problems of failing company boards, any more than they can failing university governing bodies. Sonnerfeld, a leading authority on company boards, has analysed company failures, including those of Enron, Tyco and WorldCom, and has found that many of the instant governance reforms proposed subsequently were already in place. Enron had a highly financially literate company board and a well-established audit committee; WorldCom had a big-name board with a poor attendance record but the absentee rate was similar to many very successful companies; there is no consistency of performance between companies with large or small boards. Sonnerfeld concludes that:

> The key isn't structural, its social. The most involved, diligent, value adding boards may or may not follow the good governance handbook. What distinguishes exemplary boards is that they are robust, effective social systems.
>
> (Sonnerfeld 2002)

He has listed a number of factors notably creating 'a climate of trust and candor' which offer a caution against a reliance on imposed formulaic, structural solutions to company board or governing body difficulties. 'Its not rules and regulations', he says 'it's the way people work together'. (Sonnerfeld *ibid*). A recent study by Booz Allen Hamilton suggests that just 13 per cent of US corporate failures have been caused by failures of regulatory compliance or board oversight and 87 per cent by strategic or operational error (Caulkin 2005).

Chait *et al*, writing on governance in US universities, echo these statements. On issues of size of governing body they found that their data 'safely allowed only one generalisation: large boards wished they were smaller and small boards wished they were larger' (Chait *et al* 1991). On issues of what makes boards effective, the authors listed a series of competencies beginning with:

> A board understands and takes into account the culture and norms of the organisation it governs.
>
> (Chait *et al* 1996d)

Rather than determining the mission itself as is implied by the HEC constitution.

Lay governors and a close lay involvement in university governance brings enormous benefits to academic institutions. In addition to their professional expertise in finance, the management of physical resources, or in other technical areas, lay governors have the ability to take a long view because they are not encumbered with immediate institutional management concerns, they can act as the critical friend and as the referee over internal arguments, and they can offer a reading of the environment which may be broader, and less higher education centred, than that of an institution's senior managers (Shattock 2003c). But what these contributions reflect is a need for a partnership between lay and academic governance, 'shared governance', rather than a dominant relationship between governing bodies and their senates/academic boards. Governing bodies may have the final legal power of decision-making but the most effective governing bodies exercise that power only in conjunction with the senior organs of academic governance.

5

ACADEMIC GOVERNANCE

The greater emphasis on corporate governance, the governance of universities from the top level, has tended to distract attention within higher education from governance issues lower down in the organization. But however important probity and accountability issues may be at the governing body, the overall performance of the institution is determined by what happens in academic departments, schools and faculties and by academic decisions taken by senates and academic boards. The selection and recruitment of students, home and overseas, the management of academic processes, the conduct of research, the winning of research grants and contracts, the appointment of academic staff – the processes on which the Quality Assurance Agency (QAA) audit and RAE success or failure depend – are the domain of the academic community and the forms and effectiveness of its decision-making structures provide the framework within which they take place and can determine the effectiveness of their outcomes. However, the context in which these decisions are taken has profoundly changed, and with it the organizational structures and governance processes.

Academic governance at the time of Robbins

It is worth beginning this chapter with a quotation from Sir Eric, later Lord, Ashby, a revered and establishment university figure of the 1950s and 1960s, Vice-Chancellor of Queen's University Belfast and later of Cambridge, the only UK member of Clark Kerr's Carnegie Commission on Higher Education in the US, who was both distinguished as a scientist and in later life a leading UK scholar writing

with great authority about higher education. In an essay entitled
Technology and the Academics (Ashby 1963) he wrote:

> Policy-making begins – in a healthy university at any rate – at the
> level of departments, among the teaching staff. It then rises to
> the level of the faculty where conflicting proposals from de-
> partments are reconciled in the presence of all teachers in the
> faculty. From the faculty it goes to the senate ... who reconcile
> conflicting proposals from the faculties. Only after this stage
> does it reach the council, for example, its finance and buildings
> and standing committees. Filtered through these committees,
> policy finally seeps up to the body where formal sovereignty
> resides – the council. By tradition the council only rarely alters
> any recommendations coming to it: indeed in some universities
> the statutes prevent the council from acting in academic matters
> except on the recommendation of the senate.
>
> (Ashby *ibid* a)

If the university, he wrote, 'became an institution managed by an
oligarchy instead of a society managed by its members, it would fail
to survive' (Ashby *ibid* b).

Even for Ashby this must have been an idealized picture of university governance and his vision of the vice-chancellor as:

> Far from being a man [another area where assumptions have
> changed] charged with the responsibility of creating policy, he
> finds himself obliged to feed in ideas (if he has any) at the level
> of departments or faculties and then patiently to watch them
> from the chair at numerous committees, percolating upwards
> towards the council. A large proportion of his time, and the bulk
> of his reserves of moral stamina, are spent in persuading com-
> mittees of the virtues of unanimity, guiding ideas from one
> committee to the next, and concentrating ideas into forms
> which admit of administrative action once they have been ap-
> proved by council.
>
> (Ashby *ibid* c)

was contradicted by the forceful leadership of vice-chancellors in
some civic universities in the 1950s, at Birmingham, Leeds and
Manchester, for example, who drove their institutions to expand, re-
build and develop, sometimes overcoming considerable opposition
in the process. Ashby also failed to anticipate the democratization
movements in universities in the 1960s and 1970s seeing senates as

comprising professors only, and heads of departments as being appointed until retirement.

Nevertheless these two quotations capture the principles on which university governance was based in say, 1960. Moodie and Eustace, writing a decade or so later, uncovered a much more mixed and discordant picture in their discussion of academic decision-making (Moodie and Eustace *ibid* e). Pullen, in a notably disenchanted account, describes how movement for greater representation produced the Manchester charter revision of 1973 which provided for a senate of 279 members, comprising 209 professors, *ex officio*, and 67 elected members, and which he describes as 'a flaccid body, little given to debating or voting' (Pullen 2004a). The effectiveness of the Manchester senate was tested to breaking point by the need to address the 1981 cuts and Austin's masterly account of the crucial meeting shows how the structure was simply unable to measure up to its own strategic rhetoric of concentrating resources on academic strengths and opted instead for an equitable sharing of misery amongst all departments (Austin 1982).

Academic governance and the pressure for change

Manchester's over-large senate, ill equipped for decision-making of this kind, was not, however, the only model. Newcastle had shown the way in 1962 for a slimmed-down senate which also provided for non-professorial representation, and the model statute issued by the UGC in the same year to the 1960s new universities embodied similar ideas. It is perhaps not surprising, however, that the Jarratt Committee reacted strongly against what might loosely be described as the Ashby model. The changes in context between the Robbins era of expansion and generous funding and the stringency of the early 1980s clearly required some adaptation in governance and the Jarratt commendation for a reinforcement of the role of the council and of the vice-chancellor and the establishment of a planning and resources committee represented a response to the picture painted by universities like Manchester. Anecdotally, as for example in the statement by Kenneth Durham, the Chairman of Unilever, from the same period as the Austin account:

> I gained the impression that our higher education institutions have neither the organisational structures nor as yet the management skills to deal with what will be a difficult situation in the next few years.
>
> (Durham 1982)

it was easy to conclude that the kind of situation demonstrated by Manchester was typical across UK universities. Yet not five miles away the much less celebrated Salford University was coping with budget cuts of over 40 per cent (far greater than Manchester's 16 per cent) and survived as a viable and effective institution in great part because its vice-chancellor drew on the strong organizational culture of the University to press home painful decisions which were fully agreed by a senate which could nevertheless see its membership being decimated by the results of its decisions. In practice, as Sizer's account makes clear, universities coped pretty well with what was an unprecedented reduction in income (Sizer 1987) and at least as well as other public sector bodies which suffered severe budget reductions over this period.

The climate produced by the very sharp budget reductions of the early 1980s encouraged a particular kind of reaction to university governance processes, which as we have seen above, was to have a long-lasting impact on the constitution of the polytechnics when freed from LEA control in 1988. But this climate continued to evolve, with important effects on academic governance. Middlehurst (2004) has given a convincing interpretation of the changes, basing her argument in part on earlier work by Tapper and Salter (1992). One can disagree with Tapper and Salter's case that UK universities owe their particular values to the Oxbridge model of 'the tradition of university autonomy and donnish dominion of the affairs of the university', on the grounds that such values have a universality that are not especially located in Oxbridge, but agree with their conclusion that in Middlehurst's words:

> The liberal ideal was linked both to the constitutional position of universities and to their internal operations. In constitutional terms, university autonomy and academic freedom were 'an essential pre-condition for the disinterested search for knowledge and for the preservation of those values on which a civilised society depends' (Tapper and Salter 1992). The model of internal governance that supported this position was one in which academic authority was supreme, expressed operationally in terms of management and decision-making through committees, with senior academics chairing the committees. The purpose of the committees was to achieve consensus [cf. Ashby, above] about the direction and functioning of the institution across the range of different academic interests and to maintain this over time . . . The aim was for procedures to be orderly, judgements to be carefully weighted and broad consultation to be undertaken.
>
> (Middlehurst *ibid*)

Such a situation produced slow-moving decision-making and, as Tapper and Salter suggest a form of governance which emphasized rationality and participation and which was consistent with a stable funding environment.

Middlehurst goes on to show how, drawing on Tapper and Salter, this liberal ideal has been undermined by a number of trends: the growing awareness in Government of the economic value of higher education in an internationally competitive knowledge society, the adoption by Government of a steering and evaluation role (only grasped by the UGC in its post-1980 phase), the creation of a social market where it is argued marketization and consumer choice will drive up standards, and the political belief, revived from the late 1940s and early 1950s, that the Oxbridge model is socially divisive. She argues that:

> The messages from the reports and White Papers (DES, 1987; DES, 1981; DfES, 2003) published in this twenty year period have remained broadly similar, even though the wider environment has altered significantly. 'Increase efficiency, find new sources of income and improve performance across an ever widening range of services' have been the watchwords of successive governments.
>
> (Middlehurst *ibid*)

In operational terms the financial and reputational impacts of quality assessment and the expansion in student numbers, the continuing financial stringency, the abolition of the binary line, and the increasing reliance on overseas student fees, the RAE, and the introduction of variable fees for home students, have significantly changed the dynamics of university management since the early 1980s. Middlehurst rightly argues that these conditions require further alignment of governance processes with the external environment and suggests that they have changed the focus more towards leadership and change management skills and away from internal structures and roles. Salter and Tapper in a commentary on the external pressures on institutional governance argue a second point that differentiation on the basis of research intensity has become 'a structural feature of the British university system' but the 'dominant ideological themes of higher education ... encourage the belief that all universities are homogenous in their functions – or, at least, that all have the potential to be homogenous' (Salter and Tapper 2002). If the principle of fitness for purpose is applied, they continue, then we may expect to see some differentiation in governance structures mirroring differentiation of academic mission and performance. It could be argued that a differentiation of governance styles already exists in the creation of the distinctive HEC governance structure, but in fact this was conceived as appropriate for the circumstances of 1992, as a natural development of the perspective of the Jarratt Committee, and not to complement any differentiation imposed by the RAE. To that extent it reflects 1980s thinking, and a reaction to the managerial crisis arising from the 1981 cuts in the pre-1992 universities rather than any thought of being fit for a defined purpose for the post-1992 universities.

In considering the changes in context that Middlehurst describes it is easy to forget the additional practical impact of the growth in institutional size. The Ashby model or the liberal ideal was operational in universities which regarded a 5000 student population as dangerously large. In the 1960s the University of London's 30,000 student population was only tolerable because it was managed through 25 or so separate colleges; by the late 1990s Manchester Metropolitan University had a similar student population and managed its academic governance on a unitary basis. Not only did the very rapid expansion in student numbers between 1989 and 1994 change the managerial and financial context but institutional shapes were altered by mergers – most notably by the rationalization of monotechnic teacher training colleges, and of medical schools in London – which brought with them demands for a decentralization of decision-making from overloaded governance and management structures. In the mid-1970s, when Moodie and Eustace were writing, only the collegiate universities could be described as having truly distributed sites. Most of the polytechnics, however, operated on several sites and while, since gaining university status, many have sought to consolidate their campuses the pressure of growth has often encouraged building new campuses away from the original centre of the institution. Many of the pre-1992 universities have also developed satellite campuses, as a result of mergers or the development of special facilities, and, at the extreme, some universities, both pre- and post-92, have developed off-shore campuses overseas. The growth in budgets which have accompanied these changes have necessitated significant organizational change, both from a strategic and from a control perspective, and this has necessarily been accompanied by changes in academic governance.

But another important change factor has been a new interest in higher education by Government itself. Up until the 1980s Government had regarded the universities as the private fiefdom of the UGC and had sought to intervene only rarely. With the demise of the UGC structure and a growing appreciation of the importance of research to the economy and the demand for higher level education and training in the labour force, universities found themselves increasingly subject to policy steers from Whitehall via the new funding councils. Taggart sums up the change as follows:

> in a global economy that is driven by the creation, exchange and dissemination of knowledge, the universities and colleges of higher education have become key institutions in the survival of the state; social inclusion and economic competitiveness have become twin objectives for the state in the knowledge economy and knowledge society; and higher education has become too important to be left exclusively to the higher education institutions with the consequence that higher education is increasingly, from the early 1980s onwards, managed and regulated by the state through the Department for Education and by the agent of Government, the funding body.
>
> (Taggart 2004 a)

He concludes that while 'it was once the role of Governments to provide for the purposes of the universities; it is now the role of universities to provide for the purposes of Governments' (Taggart *ibid* b). This transformation has had an important impact on institutional governance because, instead of policy-making beginning at the level of academic departments (c.f. Ashby), universities are pressured by external interventions primarily emanating from Government. The translation by the funding councils of the reports and White Papers referred to by Middlehurst above into financial incentives to embark on new functions or to expand in areas that are consonant with Government economic objectives has demanded that universities develop a decision-making machinery capable of responding. Neither councils nor senates were equipped for the task because they lacked the expertise, they met too infrequently and they were too large to make the critical decisions that were needed.

The rise of the 'strengthened steering core' ∎

In the 1960s decisions of this kind would certainly have been formulated, extensively debated and eventually taken at senate level and perhaps the most important change to take place in the civic university governance model has been the decline in the senate's engagement in critical policy formation. The academic boards in the HEC's have never, of course, aspired to assume the influence that the pre-1992 senates originally exercised. Pullen describes how, at Manchester, the senate was dominated by its standing committee

which 'predigested most of its important business' (Pullen *ibid* b).
The senate was, he says:

> inclined to rubberstamp the recommendations of most of the
> other bodies whose voluminous papers were served up to senate
> members in buff envelopes; only the most dedicated would
> skim, let alone read them all.
>
> (Pullen *ibid* c)

The device of the standing committee pre-discussing issues and
guiding an over-large and unwieldy senate was not untypical, and
persists in many institutions. But even in those universities with
'reformed', that is smaller, senates the difficulty has been to engage
senate effectively with the wider strategic issues that affect their
universities in a world where external pressures, changes in funding
policies and new Government or funding council initiatives are cumulative in effect, interrelated and demand detailed background
knowledge to be understood. Senates simply cannot meet frequently
enough to cope with the recurrent decision-making required nor
does the business, much of it detailed and bureaucratic, lend itself to
the kind of scrutiny which senate members with full teaching and
research roles are able to give. Constitutionally senates (and governing bodies) may be required formally to approve a new policy or
development but the debate, and effectively, the decision has mostly
been taken elsewhere.

It might be thought that this situation would favour the transfer of
power to a vice-chancellor in the Jarratt, chief executive mode, but
the only book-length study of the exercise of the role of a vice-
chancellor in the modern period suggests that this has not necessarily been the case. Bargh *et al* conclude that:

> Vice-chancellors regard keeping in tune with senate or academic
> board thinking as crucially important – more than one men-
> tioned in interview that those who lose their jobs do so because
> they have ceased to command the support of senate.
>
> (Bargh *et al* 2000 *ibid* b)

This is a somewhat negative assessment of the importance of consensus although the evidence of a round robin of professors at one
major university in the post-2000 period which resulted in the resignation of the incumbent might give some support to it. On the
other hand, a vote of no confidence in its vice-chancellor in another
pre-1992 university in the late 1980s led to a compensating motion
of support by the council and adverse votes at two HEC academic

boards in the 1990s, over their vice-chancellor's activities, did not precipitate immediate departures, although resignations did, in the end, take place. Generalizations, therefore, are dangerous whether in respect to universities with pre- or post-1992 constitutions because behaviour may vary according to issue and personality. The more rapid turnover of post holders in modern times – seven years is sometimes seen as a norm – has encouraged a greater variety of styles: while there are well-known cases in pre-1992 universities where vice-chancellors do act as chief executives, *strictu sensu*, and have found ways of reconciling this with the statutory powers of the senate, it is certainly the case that it is much more encouraged under an HEC constitution, where the role of the chief executive is more clearly defined and where the academic board has a more limited role in institutional governance. In the pre-1992 universities big structural academic decisions, such as the closure or merger of academic departments, must always be carried through and supported by senates for cultural as well as for statutory reasons before they can be proposed to the council, while this is not the case under the HEC articles of governance. Nevertheless, Bargh *et al* warn against simplistic linkages of managerialism at this level between the different governance structures:

> The inheritance, structures, cultures and position in the higher education firmament may be different but leadership tasks are often conceptualised in remarkably similar ways in very different institutions.
>
> (Bargh *et al ibid* c)

In fact one of the most striking changes has not been any wholesale move to a chief executive style but rather as Bargh *et al* show of vice-chancellors operating 'through and with others, whether individuals, small groups or formal committees. In short the pattern is indirect' (Bargh *et al ibid* d).

In the 1960s, vice-chancellors were remote figures even in the relatively small universities of that period: as chief administrative officer of the institution they worked closely with the registrar and/or bursar and, as the chief academic officer, they chaired the senate and its committees. By the 1970s, as Moodie and Eustace made clear, some universities were beginning to operate a 'cabinet' system but this had not been formally institutionalized even in any of the larger universities. The kind of standing committee described by Pullen was too large, too process orientated and met too infrequently to undertake this function. Vice-chancellors began with unstructured 'Monday morning meetings', with sketchy agendas and few minutes, comprising senior administrators and the one or two pro-vice-chancellors then in office but, as increasingly senates had to be asked to delegate decision-making powers between meetings to some executive body because of the pressure of issues, these Monday morning meetings became more structured with regulated membership and formal reporting-back requirements to the senate. Clark (1998) gives accounts of the roles and make up of two such bodies, the University Management Group (UMG) at Strathclyde and the Steering Committee at Warwick. In both cases these committees comprised senior academic officers, elected deans and senior administrators (at Warwick the latter were formally 'in attendance' but *de facto* were part of the decision-making process), and in both cases they reported to the governing body as necessary as well as to the senate, and had a secretary, an agenda and formal minutes like any other committee of the university. Clark described them as 'the strengthened steering core', one of the five elements of his pathways to the transformation of universities from being autonomous but passive to being self-reliant and entrepreneurial, characteristics that respond to the changed context for universities described above. Lambert quotes the UMG at Strathclyde as an example of best practice in 'collective .. executive management' (Lambert *ibid* e).

The creation of these kinds of executive body raises important organizational and constitutional issues. One of the significant distinguishing features from the senate standing committee described by Pullen is that not only do they exercise overall institutional managerial and steering roles but they are legitimized by senate to be able to communicate directly with the governing body if required, thus short-circuiting the delays imposed by only doing so through termly meetings of the senate. This gives them a managerial clout and an ability to speed up decision-making, which ensures that they play a role in all major university decisions because, in effect, they suck university business away from peripheral bodies into a cabinet-style form of governance. The membership of this cabinet tends to define the organizational character of the institution. The old Monday morning meeting might be made up of a mixed group of senior administrative and academic officers defined by seniority but would not include deans who in this organizational setting were not regarded as part of 'central management'. This was more obviously a hierarchical 'top down' structure with the deans on the outside and part of the 'managed' element of the institution. In one sense, they were one of the 'problems' that the meeting might have to wrestle with. Where this sort of Monday morning meeting became legitemized as an executive committee with defined constitutional functions, it tended to take on managerialist overtones and dealt with academic policy issues on a more arms' length basis and a separate deans committee might be given delegated powers in certain academic areas. By not including the deans, therefore, the committee becomes more obviously administrative in its remit. Where deans are included (as in the Strathclyde and Warwick examples, and in some other universities), the deans become part of the central management of the institution and, by extension, their faculties are incorporated into central decision-making. The deans thus become, not outsiders whose claims for resources or for dispensations of one kind or another have to be repelled or headed off, but part of the senior management team and, as such, sharing executive responsibility for the direction of the institution. An important advantage of this arrangement is that it brings informed discussion about academic strengths and weaknesses, problems in individual departments, and issues relating to quality reviews and RAE submissions into the centre of the university's operations.

If this represents the 'collegial' solution to the central management of universities under modern market pressures it must be recognized that many institutions have opted for a much more 'managed' approach where the senior management team act not as a cabinet but much more as a management board with an administrative manager membership. The 'Senior Executive' at DeMontfort University (described in Chapter 2) could be seen as one, perhaps extreme, example. The situation is reinforced by the adoption of the practice of regarding posts of pro-vice-chancellor or assistant vice-chancellor (and also deanships, though deans would rarely be members of this kind of management board) as appropriate for external advertisement and appointment, with full-time administrative/managerial responsibilities rather than being selected on some informal basis from within the existing cohort of staff. Pro-vice-chancellors and deans appointed on this new basis, although they may well have academic backgrounds, have essentially chosen to become full-time managers and their future performance will be judged on this basis. This sets them apart from pro-vice-chancellors and deans appointed internally, where electoral processes may play a role in the selection, and where the appointee is left space to continue some teaching or research activities, and retains the expectation of returning full time to his or her department at the conclusion of a designated period of office. Some universities also give pro-vice-chancellor or assistant vice-chancellor titles to staff with primarily professional experience such as a director of finance or of estates, or even of personnel/ human resources. These appointments are characteristic of the HECs where the explicit chief executive role of the vice-chancellor and the more restricted role of the academic board encourages a much sharper distinction between managerial and academic functions than would be the case in pre-1992 universities. Inevitably this leads to a more hierarchical top down management attitude towards academic issues than would be the case where the 'strengthened steering core' is made up substantially of people who retain a foothold in the academic community and who expect to return to it. It also changes the dynamic of the 'administration' which is more likely to be subdivided into professional groups answerable to pro-vice-chancellors or to individual senior officers who have line management responsibilities for the staff concerned, and which is much less likely to have an 'academic civil service' relationship with the academic community. Administration becomes less unitary and more organized in what Lambert describes approvingly as 'directorates' (Lambert *ibid* f) and one of the main functions of the 'management board' is to coordinate them and ensure they pull in the same direction.

Faculties and departments

Below the 'steering core', academic organizational change has also been considerable. This has been driven by the twin pressures of resource allocation theories and management fashion. For Becher and Kogan single disciplinary departments represented the basic organizational unit, that is 'the smallest component elements which have a corporate life of their own' (Becher and Kogan *ibid* a), although they accepted that in some universities faculties or schools of studies fulfilled this role. One of the unacknowledged problems of modern university governance is how to connect these basic units, from which Ashby believed key policies emerged, to the central decision-making machinery made necessary by the new policy environment and by the demands of institutional size and diversity. To what extent are they partners and to what extent subordinate entities? Since their performance, whether in relation to the recruitment and teaching of students or in relation to the RAE, is critical to institutional success, financial and academic, what mechanisms of evaluation, intervention and control should the central decision-making machinery maintain and engage in on behalf of the institution as a whole? Should these mechanisms be merely financial and hands off or should they be academic and hands on or some combination of the two and how do these different approaches impact on the role and the constitutional position of departments? What intermediary machinery lies between the central decision-making bodies and the departments – is it a faculty board led by an elected dean or chair, where the financial relationships are direct between the department and the centre, or is it a faculty board with an appointed dean who is the budget holder for a group of departments or schools?

These and related questions have had a profound influence on the status of faculties and departments within institutional governance structures. In particular the transparency of funding council resource allocation processes introduced in the 1980s prompted a revolution in the way individual institutions approached internal resource allocation to departments or faculties. If the composition of the institutional funding package could be broken down into its constituent parts and rebuilt into a departmental or faculty budget calculation the resource allocation process had to be robust if it were to justify variations from the transparent model in funding between different basic units. Senates were not always strong enough to resist a reversion to formula funding which mirrored the funding councils' own formulae. When this happened the assumption that there was an entitlement often grew up, making it more difficult for the centre to shift resources around to invest in future success or, in the telling phrase, 'cross-subsidize' financially weaker areas. This loosens the sense of interdependence between the centre and some of the larger basic units and reinforces departmental/school faculty autonomy and a more balkanized structure Whereas the pre-1992 universities took time and a good deal of experimentation, especially bearing in mind the importance of RAE funding, to adjust to the new funding arrangements the HECs inherited from the 1988 Act, when they were freed from local authority control, the need to generate resources by attracting additional student numbers, and this encouraged management structures where deans of faculties were given devolved budgets which were dependent on their faculties' abilities to meet student number targets. In most HECs deans were accountable for balancing their books, almost irrespective of what financial teaming and ladling had to be undertaken between departments.

In a period of acute financial stringency it is perhaps not surprising that resource allocation processes often created the framework which defined relationships between the centre and the basic units and how these could vary between institutions. Jarzabkowski's account of centralized and decentralized resource allocation models at Warwick, LSE and Oxford Brookes shows how the very 'hands on' peer group evaluation from the centre at Warwick built exceptionally close links and common strategic approaches between departments and the centre, while the strategic planning cycle allocation to budget centres, offered a contrasting and much more 'hands off' and bureaucratic relationship at Oxford Brookes (Jarzabkowski 2002). As the concepts of transparency and formula funding became more developed, these relationships became further defined by the concept of budget centres paying a *juste retour* to the centre, normally calculated at around 40 per cent of the budget centre's turnover. Thus the relationship between the centre and the academic units tended in some universities to become primarily financial. Change was often driven by management fashion and the philosophy that decisions were better made the closer they were to the coalface. In a big university with 50 or so departments a resource allocation process based on that number of basic units, often units which were themselves uneconomically small, was also found to be inefficient and time consuming, and allocations to faculties or schools linked to overall strategic guidance from the centre passed responsibility down the line where, it was argued, it could be exercised more effectively. In many universities the trigger for such changes was a change of vice-chancellor and a belief that a change in organizational structure, often lifted wholesale from the incoming vice-chancellor's old university, would automatically improve the university's RAE and other prospects. The danger was that such changes, to make them acceptable, were simply grafted on to existing structures so that universities increased their internal bureaucracy rather than simplified it (for example see the University D case study in Chapter 6).

Since, in an RAEIY and league table-conscious university world, selection committees want to appoint vice-chancellors who will improve the institution's standing, the pace of academic reorganization has accelerated. Hogan has provided some surprising figures as to the extent of academic reorganizations that have taken place (Hogan 2005). His research concludes that between 1993 and 2002, out of 81 universities in his survey, '60 (74%) appear to have undertaken at least one significant academic reorganisation during the nine year period. Only two of the post-1992 universities ... did not undergo a significant academic reorganisation' (Hogan *ibid*). The extent of these reorganizations can be judged from his analysis: reduction in both the number of faculties and departments (18), reduction in the number of faculties/schools (11), increase in the number of faculties/schools and reduction in the number of departments (3); reduction in the number of faculties/schools and increase in the number of departments (2); reorganization of their faculties (3); removal of faculties altogether and replacement with departments merged into schools (3); or simply a reduction in the number of faculties or departments (7). In addition 12 universities increased their number of faculties or departments. Hogan provides further evidence in a separate analysis that 51 out of 68 universities had changed their academic structure of faculties or schools between 1994 and 2002, 26 reducing the number of faculties, 12 replacing faculties with schools, two replacing schools with faculties, and 11 increasing the number of faculties/schools. Hogan particularly notes the reorganization of a number of civic universities: Birmingham, Edinburgh, Newcastle, Nottingham and Southampton had all reorganized a large number of departments into schools, with Edinburgh and Newcastle also merging their faculties into quasi 'colleges' with provosts or super-deans at their heads; Oxford had devolved day-to-day decision-making to five academic divisions that were superimposed on the existing faculty structure; at Manchester the decision to merge the University with the Manchester Institute of Science and Technology offered the opportunity for dramatic compositing of faculty structures, to which, as at Edinburgh and Newcastle, substantial elements of what were previously central administrative and decision-making functions, were also devolved. Perhaps an extreme form of devolution can be illustrated by an advertisement for the post of Principal of the Faculty of Life Sciences at Imperial College, a faculty which has four divisions (Biology, Cell and Molecular Biology, Molecular Biological Sciences and Biomedical Sciences) and a Centre for Environmental Policy. The Principal is required to 'provide intellectual leadership, direction and motivation across the divisions' to manage the divisional heads, recruit potential staff worldwide, and identify 'new research prospects and opportunities for interdisciplinary collaboration as well as new sources of "third stream" funding' and also to be a key member of the College's senior management team (*Times Higher Education Supplement* 2005). This could be seen as the 'business' model for faculty management.

In reviewing the rationale for the changes Hogan quotes some representative examples: at Northumbria, where a reorganization followed the arrival of a new vice-chancellor, five faculties and 15 departments were replaced by 11 schools 'to enhance communication and efficiency across the organisation' (University of Northumbria 2002 quoted in Hogan *ibid* a), while at Edinburgh the reorganization into 21 schools in three colleges was 'to permit efficient and effective management of resources' (University of Edinburgh 2001 quoted in Hogan *ibid* b). As Hogan demonstrates 'The direction of most of this academic reorganisation has been towards a smaller number of bigger units' (Hogan *ibid* c), but 'There is no consensus on the correct organisational arrangement of academic disciplines in universities' (Hogan *ibid d*) and he concludes that this suggests 'that managerial rather than academic concerns have been dominant factors behind most reorganisations' (Hogan *ibid* d). Certainly there have been contradictory movements. Thus Leicester embarked on a devolution of resource allocation decisions to deans in 1996 under one vice-chancellor but reverted to a centralized centre to academic department process under his replacement five years later. While Sussex, against what could be seen as a national trend, as demonstrated, for example, at Birmingham where departments were rationalized into schools as a concomitant to sweeping away a previous faculty structure that had devolved resource allocation powers, took the decision to abandon its historic commitment to schools, and revert to academic departments. But these reflect individual circumstances, as well as different perceptions of what might be the nature of the structural problem. Whereas at Birmingham the decision to remove the faculties and their extensive administrative support represented substantially a de-layering to reduce costs, at Leicester and Sussex, universities which were both anxious to retain their research intensive status, the decisions were geared to improving their RAE position: at Leicester resource allocation by deans had not been effective; at Sussex the school structure was thought to be insufficiently robust to match RAE logic.

There is no doubt that much structural change has been driven by a too easy acceptance of 'the grass is greener' syndrome – university X is doing better than us; it must be because of their academic structure. But there have been other forces at work as well. The post-Robbins expansion in the pre-1992 universities led to a wholesale establishment of new departments and degree programmes, particularly in the arts and social sciences and particularly in the older civic universities, leaving universities with many small departments that they had expected would grow to a mature size. The UGC's 1979 report on Russian Studies, which recommended the closure of courses or departments at six universities and the possible phasing out of Russian Studies at seven more argued that there were academic advantages in fewer but larger groups. These were the ability to have a wider range of courses, a more favourable atmosphere for research, better library facilities, improved opportunities for study leave and 'greater effective weight (or less vulnerability) in the local allocation of resources' (quoted in Shattock 1994a). Broadly similar conclusions were reached for the earth sciences by the Oxburgh report in 1987 which categorized earth sciences departments into those suitable for research and teaching, those for teaching and those that should simply be contributing individual courses to other degree programmes. Only three departments had more than 25 staff, compared to the US where four out of five of the most highly ranked departments were of this size (quoted in Shattock 1994b). These two reports, widely criticized at the time, were also highly influential in internal university decision-making especially as the RAE processes gathered weight and a sense of permanence. But universities adopted different approaches to the governance issues surrounding the decision-making to which RAE logic pointed. One was to take on the rationalization exercise required at the central committee level, through a Jarratt-style planning and resources committee; another was to devolve the budget to a faculty or to a school structure, leaving the pressure on resources at that level to be the driver for rationalization. Jarzabkowski, in her account of resource allocation models, shows how the Warwick 'hands on' approach and the Oxford Brookes 'hands off' approach successfully coped with these kinds of decisions (Jarzabkowski *ibid*).

If research was one driver, changes in teaching arrangements represented a further unstated force for changes in academic organization. Watson's *Managing the Modular Course* (Watson 1989) had already given encouragement to polytechnics to embark on what became later known as the 'modularization and semesterization' of courses in polytechnics and in 1991 a Committee of Vice-Chancellors and Principals' (CVCP) paper entitled 'Modular Curriculum and Structure' urged its adoption in the universities citing *inter alia* the advantages of improving 'the quality/economy of teaching/learning flexibility to accommodate an increasing diversity of entrant' and increasing 'the number of pathways through the total provision of an institution' (quoted in Shattock 2003d). Whether or not these advantages have been realized in the adoption of modularization in many pre-1992 and most post-1992 universities, modularity itself has had the effect of breaking down departmental boundaries that preserved the mono-disciplinary degree programme and has provided an additional legitimization of the school idea where a group of related departments are encompassed within a single decision-making unit.

All these pressures have placed the concept of the department as the basic unit in a university's organizational structure in many institutions at risk; and even if it is not actually at risk, as institutions have grown larger, departments find themselves further and further away from a fast-moving decision-making process. Bolton argues that widespread cynicism is the natural result of the perception in a department that the centre has taken decisions without consulting it on matters on which it has a legitimate interest (Bolton *ibid* a). In many cases what a department might regard itself as having a legitimate interest in can be a fairly elastic concept, so in reorganizing academic structures universities which base their academic governance on participative processes need to weigh up the length of the communication systems involved between the centre and the basic units, give consideration to formal and informal representation mechanisms and recognize the pivotal role of the dean in bridging the inevitable consultation gaps. Where participative structures are regarded as less important, either because a more formal managerial structure is preferred or because of factors of institutional size or physical dispersal, these communication systems may be considered much less important and an explicit devolved structure in budgetary as well as academic organizational terms may be more appropriate. But the danger inherent in devolution to a faculty-based structure is the creation of an additional layer of academic governance which, because it is necessarily close to the departments or schools which it resources, is less likely to be as clear sighted in its strategic approach to resource allocation and more likely to be influenced by considerations of having to observe faculty perceptions of the importance of the range of disciplines it represents relative to other faculties (chemistry is just more important to the nation's future than the arts and must therefore be preserved) than a centrally determined process. On the other hand, the danger inherent in a centralized structure is that the centre loses touch with the basic units and comes to be seen as arbitrary and insensitive in its decision-making. Both dangers can be mitigated by an energetic dean, who can channel information both ways, but to do this effectively, the dean must be part of the institution's central decision-making process, representing the faculty view there as well as representing the institutional strategic view to the faculty and department.

Webber provides an interesting discussion of the issues involved. Drawing on Williams (1992) he suggests that:

> The 'devolution solution' offered a way of accelerating and streamlining systems by shortening decision-making chains, building local 'ownership' of the decision-making process, enabling decisions themselves to be more sensitive to local knowledge and making local decision-makers more clearly and directly responsible for the consequences of those decisions.
>
> (Webber 1998a)

But, he continues, devolution raises a series of questions: 'What precisely should be devolved? To whom exactly? At what level(s) in the hierarchy? On what basis? And with what controls?' (Webber *ibid* b). He concludes:

> It was always clear that different combinations of answers to these questions would have different consequences for the way that organisations worked. Unfortunately, experience suggests that all too often universities focused more on the details than on the consequences of their choices.
>
> (Webber *ibid* c)

These consequences may involve mergers of departments into

schools or the loss of departmental budgetary autonomy to executive deans, or, more significant for the university as a whole, a change in the approach to resource allocation to a formulaic allocation to faculty-based academic groupings. They may also involve the adoption of financial rather than academic criteria in associated decision-making. The theory of devolved budgeting, for example, is that it encourages innovation and entrepreneurialism at local levels but resource allocation from a smaller devolved budget may in fact be more cautious and more based on financial considerations than if undertaken at the institutional level. Clark Kerr suggests that universities, like industry, have a standard pattern of reorganization:

> to decentralise too much and, when this did not work, to recentralise too much, and when this did not also work, to change again – a yo yo process in perpetuity.
>
> (Kerr 2001)

Perhaps case study University E (Chapter 6) represents a forerunner of this process in the UK.

Academic organization and the governance of academic structures are under-researched subjects and simplistic notions that improvements can be obtained by a simple carryover of a structure from one institution to another are fraught with difficulty. Financial logic or the streamlining of academic decision-making may point unerringly towards merging departments into multi-disciplinary schools, but the persistent congruity of disciplinary groups may leave those departments effectively intact, meeting to defend their discipline against others, and creating complex political situations which the chair of the school finds difficult to resolve and to represent in faculty-wide decision-making. Against this the flatter structure of resource allocation direct to departments may, in larger universities, become so formulaic that it loses the strategic value of the direct relationship between the basic unit and the centre of the university. The level of research intensity, the disciplinary mix, location on a single or on several institutional sites, or the danger of shortfalls in student numbers in particular areas may all influence academic structures and the appropriate levels at which key academic and/or financial decisions should be taken. What is important is that such structures should not be adopted simply for financial convenience but to fit an academic strategy and that they should be monitored to be sure they deliver what is expected of them and not be maintained simply for reasons of *amour propre*. Academic structures that do not work can raise tensions, make difficult decisions constitutionally even more difficult to make and can render the working lives of the academics who are appointed to teach and research more or less fulfilling. An effective academic structure, one that is seen to be permeable to ideas from the bottom and receptive to ideas from the top, makes a significant contribution to creating a positive organizational culture; a structure which is dislocated or which has internal contradictions may severely inhibit institutional progress. As Hogan says: 'No matter what direction [a] reorganisation takes, it is bound to involve a period of disruption or uncertainty as the previous structures are replaced' (Hogan *ibid* e). Universities may need to recognize that making a structure work better by small evolutionary changes is more effective and involves fewer distractions from creative academic work than fundamental academic reorganizations. In a decade and a half of significant academic reorganization there are few, if any, examples of universities that can positively adduce improved RAE scores or better student recruitment as identifiable outcomes of major structural change. Most reorganizations are, in fact, defensive in inspiration, intended to prevent further slippage, improve accountability, eliminate weaknesses and remove inefficiencies, rather than to buttress strengths. While this may reflect accurately the continued reduction of the unit of resource which universities have faced over this period it is not surprising that changes of academic structure have often seemed threatening to those they affect and have done little for academic morale.

Academic governance structures need to be designed first and foremost to conduct academic business effectively, to deliver academic views and decisions upwards, to report discussions and decisions taken by central bodies downwards and to facilitate debate on university issues generally. We should not be surprised when faculty boards or departments resist change or rationalization: what is important is that they are given all the relevant facts which will be available to higher bodies in making their decision to consider and that the processes of decision-making are open and transparent. Academic structures will vary between universities depending on circumstances and disciplinary base; almost certainly the most effective will be the one that most academics and administrators are the most comfortable with.

Senates/academic boards

While substantial reorganizations in academic structures in respect to faculties, schools and departments have been initiated, too little attention has been given to the role of senates and academic boards. Partly this is because they have to some extent been supplanted by senior executive management groups and partly because the increasing pressures of academic accountability and legal interventions over academic processes have come to occupy a great deal of their time. In universities with civic university constitutions senate meetings are less well attended and do not attract senior academics who have a broad interest in university matters; they are often criticized by their members because the body has become a rubber stamp for decisions taken by the senior executive management group, only becoming fully engaged in strictly local disputes. Some of the reasons for this are referred to above page 65), but one at least is the unwieldy nature of the senates themselves. Where governing bodies have had to address reform because it has been pressed on them so vigorously from outside, senates and academic boards have generally continued unchanged, often with over large memberships, committee structures which deliver decisions too slowly and an unwillingness to dispatch decisions in a business-like way. Conscientious academics pressured by worsening staff/student ratios and RAE demands, like busy lay members of governing bodies, face time constraints which are difficult to reconcile with over long, underdisciplined meetings. In many universities it could be argued that over two decades the senate has changed from being a key operational element in university governance to being part of the 'dignified' apparatus of governance, a safety valve rather than a positive element in the decision-making process. The long-term effect of this must be a weakening of corporate self-belief, and, while a quiescent senate may be a comfort to a vice-chancellor facing hard choices, it represents a lower commitment to institutional autonomy and corporate responsibility for strategic decisions. Senates that believe in maintaining a balance in the power relationship with governing bodies, as envisaged in their statutes, need to follow the devices to encourage their members' engagement of induction programmes, self-scrutiny and performance review which are now routine at the governing body level, in order to ensure that they are capable of playing the role in governance that their constitutional powers offer them.

Much more important in modern university governance than structure is good communication, trust and a sense of participation in decision-making either institutionally or at least at the level of the basic unit. It is inevitable and right that as pressures change, flexible organizations will change with them. The relative turmoil of organizational change identified by Hogan could be seen positively as a sign of adaptability to a changing external environment. Too few universities have faced up to the need to reform their senates/academic boards in order that they can respond quickly to the needs of working in partnership with their reformed governing bodies, but it is likely that senates/academic boards are themselves only going to be effective bodies when major issues of principle or practice need decision and when much of the detail they often concern themselves with is delegated to subsidiary bodies or to individuals. In modern conditions, the day-to-day decision-making which maintains the institution's operational effectiveness and which keeps it competitive will have to be devolved to the central steering mechanism described above. That in itself is less significant, providing this mechanism works well, than that it combines managerial grip with an appropriate representational dimension and that it communicates well with its academic constituents in a way which convinces them that it is to be trusted as a body to take sensible decisions both academic and financial on their behalf, and that it is answerable, in the end, to the senate/academic board and to the governing body for doing so. Streamlined faculties and departmentally grouped schools can work well if they appear to be aligned with the institution's academic priorities and strategies, but can prove to be a constraint on the effective conduct of business if they simply serve as mechanisms that cloak older disciplinary divisions or drive such divisions underground. In many universities, the department will remain the natural unit and efforts to deny this will simply add extra layers to the decision-making process and greatly lengthen the lines of communication. Universities remain people-intensive businesses and do not respond well to an imposed hierarchy which elevates structure, of itself, to be an organizing principle.

The student role in governance

The Scottish ancient universities have an entirely different tradition of the involvement of students in university governance to the rest of the UK (Ashby and Anderson 1970) and the relics of this remain in the appointment of the rector, a position elected by the student body, which formally has the right to chair meetings of the university governing body, the court. Since the late 1980s the head of the institution has relinquished the role of chair to a senior lay member, thus bringing Scotland into line with England and Wales, but these historic arrangements, in theory, entrench students in university goverance structures in a more radical way than anywhere else in the UK.

In 1974, as a result of the student activism of the late 1960s and early 1970s, the CVCP and the National Union of Students reached a concordat over student representation in university governance on a

UK basis. The effect of this was to bring student membership onto all governing bodies and senates and academic boards, and in many universities onto faculty boards, subject to their exclusion in respect to the personal affairs of staff or students. This practice was adopted by the polytechnics and this extended to the post-1992 universities. (The Huddersfield case study in Chapter 6 recounts where a university sought to renege on this.) While in the 1970s the introduction of student membership was thought likely to inaugurate a considerable increase in student involvement in governance issues, the opposite has rather been the case, except in specifically local issues where student union policies have collided with a university's. Even the change in recurrent grant rules, when the previously identified element for student activities, a *per capita* sum which the university normally handed over to fund students union activities, was absorbed into the recurrent grant in the 1980s, failed to raise the level of student engagement with university affairs at the senior levels of governance. On the other hand, all universities encouraged the establishment of departmental student/staff liaison committees and these have become the main conduit for dialogue on academic matters. Two external actions have given these committees added importance: the first was the decision to include the student voice in formal Quality Assurance processes, to the extent that in the Teaching Quality Assurance (TQA) reviews, departments could be asked to provide copies of the minutes of staff–student meetings from the last three years; the second has been the introduction of the National Student Survey and the publication of the results as league tables in the media.

It was always assumed that once students had to pay fees they would choose to exercise a greater consumerist role within higher education resulting in an enhanced representative role in university government, but the introduction of fees for home students in 2000 brought no recognizable change in student attitudes, just as the introduction of full-cost fees for overseas students in 1981 failed to create the consumerist pressures on university campuses that might have been expected. However, the results of the first round of National Survey of Student Attitudes has undoubtedly led to a much heightened sense of institutional dependence on student opinion and seems set fair to encourage a much stronger involvement at all levels in university governance. At the time of writing it is too soon to anticipate how this might develop.

6

GOVERNANCE BREAKDOWNS AND ISSUES

As we have seen there is a tendency, particularly in the corporate world, to regard observing the forms of governance primarily as providing reassurance to investors and shareholders. In part this is justified because prescribed governance processes form organizational behaviour patterns and because the requirement to report the machinery of governance in the formal accounts and where there are variations from established norms, imposes on directors (or members of university governing bodies) the responsibility of signing up to them and on auditors the need to inquire into whether the report represents a true picture. The danger, as the Hampel Report makes clear, is that ticking the good governance boxes becomes a substitute for good management and good decision-making processes. One of the great values of the TransTec Report was that it described a corporate governance failure caused by the 'passive' culture of the board, the extent to which its processes were informal and sloppy and the way it was dominated by its successive chief executives, who kept the non-executive directors at arm's length from the executive directors and from the rest of the management team. (Aldous and Kaye 2003 *ibid*). The board could have ticked most of the good governance boxes but would still have been defective as a body.

Governance breakdowns may be procedural, in the sense that rules have been broken or governance norms have been ignored, but we should not delude ourselves into ignoring the fact that such actions are the product of acts of omission or commission by individuals, of failures of judgement, of professional competence or simply of lack of thought for the likely consequences. Governance and management are always closely interlocked and management failure is as often the trigger for governance failure as the other way round.

Perhaps the greatest test of a governance structure is where a board or governing body determines that it cannot support its chief executive in a particular set of circumstances. As we shall see from some of the university cases described below, such breakdowns generally occur too late when a governing body has gone along with much that individual members may have been unhappy with because it is over-dependent for advice and expertise on the vice-chancellor or one of the senior officers. There must always be a tendency for boards, as in the case of TransTec, and university governing bodies, to trust the advice they are given and the problem is mostly about at what point this trust breaks down. A board or governing body that continuously questioned small decisions or demanded reassurance on minor issues would soon immobilize the institution it served and demoralize its executive staff. Inevitably, there has to be a certain suspension of disbelief, and governing bodies, made up essentially, as we have seen, of unpaid non-executives are unlikely to spot trends quickly enough to recognize that a sequence of decisions may be leading the institution in the wrong direction. Universities only occasionally take 'big decisions', such as to open a campus overseas, or to close a major department, and on those occasions it would be likely that the issues would be debated extensively at senates/ academic boards and at governing bodies. Much more often universities are positioned by sequences of small decisions, perhaps spread over several years, or by inattention to or complacency towards key operations which are then difficult to redress quickly. Thus management and governance go hand in hand, and since universities do not have relatively simple and universally recognizable measures of comparison such as profitability, shareholder value or return on capital, any slippage of performance is difficult to identify within the governance structures even if it is recognized very clearly by some sections of the management. Even the most obvious indicator of the need for concern, a long-run deficit situation, can be dressed up as a necessary phase while investment bears fruit because the bottom line is not necessarily viewed as the sovereign or even the most relevant performance indicator for an academic institution.

Yet, as we shall see, in some of the cases below, cumulative bad decision-making at several governance levels within the institution, either because they dig not dig deeply enough for the right data or because the data was not there or was obscured, coupled with headstrong or ineffective management, brought institutions to crisis points. While this points strongly to the need for effective performance review conducted, not solely at governing body level but jointly with senates/academic boards, performance review cannot be seen as an instant panacea because poorly performing institutions will often have ineffective governance structures and weak management which will fail to recognize or will deliberately ignore telltale signs of corporate decline with spurious rhetoric.

Some of the case studies outlined below deal exclusively with crises in governance, but we need to recognize that these crises often reflected or came about from a need to rectify long-run management failure. Poor management and ineffective governance are intertwined; good governance practice may eliminate some of the grosser failures but it will not always, or even very often, address the 80 per cent of the iceberg which lies below the waterline. Where academic staff have risen up and protested in votes of no confidence it is often because they can see some of this 80 per cent which revealed shortcomings which were much less evident, if evident at all, to the governing body. Good governance is not, therefore, the prerogative of only one body, but must run through the institution.

Other cases illustrate how governing bodies and chief executives acted together to pursue policy objectives that were not endorsed by the wider academic community, where governing bodies were ineffective in controlling the inappropriate behaviour of the chief executive or where a governing body itself made inappropriate decisions in respect to the remuneration of its chief executive. In all these cases, it is important to bear in mind the management context; governance breakdowns occurred because weak or ineffective governance structures were put under too much strain or where they were forced to act because of external pressures. Some other cases are designed to show how governance practice at levels below the governing body can contribute to or depress institutional performance. Here, of course, we are not talking about governance breakdowns that hit the headlines and brought institutions to their knees, but about governance problems in the academic heartlands which inhibited institutional performance, caused internal difficulties, and reduced efficiency and effectiveness. Left to fester such problems may affect the long-term position of the institution in even more serious ways.

Notes on the case studies

Where the cases have been made public through publication (normally in the form of a published report or a Public Accounts Committee hearing), the names of the case study institutions are shown because they are readily identifiable and the sources for the account are listed. It is important to recognize that in all these cases subsequent reforms have been made and the institutions have re-emerged as effectively governed and managed; these case studies should be treated as illustrations of what can go wrong rather than any form of indictment of the institutions as they now present themselves. Where there has been no public report institutions are not mentioned by name; these cases represent institutions where the author himself has had some involvement or special knowledge and are again quoted to illustrate issues in governance and not to reflect on the effectiveness of the institutions as they now operate. None of the case studies purports to offer an overall account of the particular set of issues but only to identify 'real-life' cases of what might be described as generic problems in university governance.

Governance and financial decision-making

University College, Cardiff

The Cardiff case set the scene for much of what was to follow in the UK in terms of making institutions more directly accountable for the expenditure of public money and creating the regulatory framework within which responsibility could be directly laid on and accepted by governance structures. It is therefore important not just for the case itself but for the impact it has had on relations between the university system and the Department of Education and Science (DES, now the Department for Education and Skills, DfES) and on the audit and other mechanisms of accountability, including the Financial Memorandum referred to in Chapter 3. In 1986, when the problems at Cardiff first hit the headlines, the permanent secretary of the DES was the accounting officer for the university system but, under convention, acted on the advice of the chairman of the UGC. The UGC saw its role as ensuring that 'each individual university institution should be left to manage its own affairs with the minimum of detailed instructions' (UGC 1973). By 1989, as a direct result of the Cardiff affair, the chief executive of the new Universities Funding Council (UFC) had become designated the accounting officer, the Financial Memorandum had been created along with new audit regulations, internal audit and audit committees had become institutional requirements and the Funding Council had direct access to institutional audit reports.

University College, Cardiff, now Cardiff University, was the premier university institution in Wales. Although formally a constituent college of the University of Wales, it received its recurrent grant direct from the UGC, and while its degrees were those of the University of Wales, it was in every other respect an independent university. It had the traditional governance structure of a pre-1992 university with a council and a senate and was led by a dominant principal who had played a significant role since his appointment in 1967 in raising the institution's academic standing. Within the city of Cardiff there was another university institution, the University of Wales Institute of Science and Technology (UWIST); a merger of the two institutions had been formally agreed in principle with the UGC but was in practice strongly resisted by the principal and by his council and senate. The principal acted very much in the Jarratt mould as a chief executive and commanded the full support of his council. The chairman of the finance and general purposes committee, who had the title of university treasurer, took pride in the brevity of his committee's meetings as an indicator of its efficiency. The senate was rather less compliant, but was in support of the principal and the council in its scepticism as to the value of a merger with UWIST. The college had a registrar, who was also deputy principal and professor of classics, and a bursar, who had previously worked for the Arts Council of Wales; neither was effective as a manager and both were wholly under the sway of the principal.

Cardiff had suffered a modest 7 per cent reduction in its budget (as compared to the average of around 15 per cent) in the UGC's programme of cuts in the 1981–84 period. It did not, however, make the kind of economies that other universities undertook: it created an early retirement scheme that was enormously expensive, the finance committee accepting without question a complex document explaining the scheme when it was laid on the table of the meeting; academic departments, while formally given budgets, were allowed to overspend at will on the grounds that their heads knew better than the finance office what the appropriate level of expenditure should be. The College went into deficit in 1981–82 and remained there each year. In 1984–85 the treasurer reassured the council that 'the College's current financial difficulties were of a purely temporary nature and would be readily resolved by the adjustments now being made' (Committee of Public Accounts 1990).

Two other areas may be quoted as examples, among many, where governance machinery designed to exercise financial control was either circumvented or ignored. Procedures for senior staff appointments and promotions were prescribed in a staff handbook, yet in 1982 five promotions of administrative staff to the most senior (professorial-equivalent) salary grade were agreed by the finance committee, without justifying papers, under an agenda item entitled 'principal's business'. In 1963 the principal directed the registrar to appoint a college appeal organizer to a half-time post of consultant at a professorial equivalent salary. No contract was ever issued; the appeal never covered its costs. In 1985 the person appointed was made full-time director of the new China Studies Centre, again without committee authority or academic scrutiny; the Centre was closed in 1987 having recruited no students. Procedures for capital expenditure were similarly lax and purchases and sales of property, mostly at a loss, were authorized by the principal and carried out by the bursar without reportage to the finance committee. In one case, however, the purchase of a new telephone exchange, there appears to have been a full committee involvement. In 1981 a senate committee had proposed the creation of a sinking fund to purchase a new telephone exchange and asked the bursar and the principal to report back to it; this was agreed but no purchase was made and no sinking fund created. Two years later the committee reminded itself that no report back had occurred but that the telephone system was becoming increasingly obsolescent and, in 1985, the council appointed consultants to advise on the design, procurement and installation of the new system. Their report prompted a paper to the finance committee that the installation of a new system would reduce the telephone bill by over £200,000, figures not included in the consultants' report, and the finance committee went ahead with expenditure of £850,000 on the stated basis that the savings would give a payback of five to six years on investment. No sinking fund was ever set up. This capital expenditure was undertaken when the College accounts for 1984–85 showed an accumulated deficit of £3.5 million and an overdraft on 31 July 1985 of £3.2 million. The actual payback in the first year was estimated at £107,000. The designated council committee thus failed to exercise proper control and the council itself, although aware of the overall financial situation, failed to safeguard the College's position.

In late 1985 the College's 1984–85 accounts became available to the UGC which advised the permanent secretary of its concern at the deteriorating financial situation. The permanent secretary called for a report from the accountants, Price Waterhouse. Their report, compiled without the cooperation of the College's auditors (who put loyalty to the College council above the requirements of public accountability), forecast further deficits in 1985–86 and 1986–87 and a rising cumulative deficit. The council disputed the report forecasting a surplus in 1986–87 and a much lower cumulative deficit, and in a formal response to the permanent secretary criticized the report as being 'unsound' and 'not based on fact' and committed itself to the view that its plans were 'realistic' and provided 'the basis for planning for the rest of the decade' (quoted in Shattock 1994c). Subsequent investigation on behalf of the UGC showed the forecast recurrent and cumulative deficits as being likely to be even higher than reported by Price Waterhouse. In late 1986 the senate recorded its lack of confidence in the financial management of the College and the following month it passed a vote of no confidence in the principal, a vote that was rejected by the council. In February 1987 the senate met again under the principal's chairmanship. He withdrew while his position was discussed and the minute records:

> After discussion *it was resolved* that the Principal be asked not to exercise his right to chair meetings of the Senate. Having been informed of this resolution by the Deputy Principal (Humanities) (that is the Registrar) the Principal returned to the meeting and informed the Senate that he intended to exercise his right to chair its meetings.
>
> (quoted in Smith and Cunningham 2003)

Providing he retained the confidence of council the senate was impotent. But in the same month the permanent secretary suspended the College's recurrent grant subject to the council accepting a team designated by the UGC. By this time the College's overdraft limit with its bankers was within a hair's breadth of being breached, which had it been would have produced the unprecedented appointment of a receiver in a UK university. One immediate result was the removal from office of the principal, the registrar and the bursar.

The subsequent rescue of Cardiff and the merger with UWIST has been recounted elsewhere but what makes Cardiff, even after the lapse of a considerable time, such an important case study is as follows:

- The extent to which its governance, at the level of its council and its council committees, became simply the sounding board for a headstrong chief executive and were unable to exercise any independent financial judgement until he himself had been removed from office.
- There was no audit committee which could advise the council separately from the principal; the external auditors were not themselves truly independent or they would have alerted the council and would have collaborated with Price Waterhouse.
- The absence of any effective control on the Principal from the designated officers and in particular from the registrar whose role as secretary to the council and the senate should have required him to report his concerns, if he had any, at least to the lay officers; he should have insisted that proper procedures be followed in regard to staff appointments and promotions and to capital expenditure. He was compromised in this by his role as Deputy Principal.

- The interrelationship between governance failure and management failure over a range of operations – there was no one major decisive failure which brought the university down but it was the cumulative effect of bad financial decision-making over many areas over a long period; the governance/management interface was subverted by a powerful Principal – a strong governance structure at both senate and council levels could have ensured financial control.

- The senate did not challenge the Principal over his handling of the 1981 budget reductions even though it must have been obvious to many senior academics that optimism about various schemes for income generation was not sustainable; a closer relationship between council and senate might have prompted more questioning of individual financial actions.

- There was no recognition at a senior level in the institution that it was responsible for the financial control of expenditure of public money, and that it was ultimately answerable to Parliament through the Comptroller and Auditor General and the Public Accounts Committee for the misapplication of such funds; in effect it behaved as if it was private money which it received as of right.

Sources: Shattock, M.L. (1987) *Report on the Implementation of Financial Control at University College, Cardiff*, UGC (unpublished); Shattock, M.L. (1988) 'Financial Management in Universities: the lessons from University College, Cardiff' *Financial Management and Accountability* 4(2); Shattock, M.L. (1994) *The UGC and the Management of British Universities*, Buckingham: Open University Press, Chapter 6 'Financial Accountability and the Cardiff Affair'; Smith, B. and Cunningham, V. (2003) 'Crisis in Cardiff' in Warner, D. and Palfreyman, D. (eds) *Managing Crisis*, Maidenhead: Open University Press; personal knowledge of the author.

The University of Lancaster

The University was a 1960s' 'new university' which achieved good research ratings in the 1989 RAE and even better in the 1992. Student numbers had doubled in the 1980s and, with the RAE success, further expansion was being planned for. The vice-chancellor who had been appointed in 1985 from MIT (Massachusetts Institute of Technology) was due to retire in 1995. The crisis which hit the University in 1995–96 was caused by serious cash flow shortfalls caused by an over-ambitious building programme which had got out of control. So concerned was the academic community at the governance and management failures endemic in this affair that it commissioned its own review of what had gone wrong and, to its credit, published it (Rowe 1997).

The University had a traditional council and senate, but following a review in 1993 introduced a new committee structure: the finance committee's remit was widened to become a finance and general purposes committee, chaired by a lay non-executive treasurer, and the small academic planning committee, a post-Jarratt joint committee of council and senate, was converted into an academic planning board to be chaired by the vice-chancellor which was to have two sub-committees, a budget and monitoring committee and an estates committee, both chaired by pro-vice-chancellors; the former buildings committee of the council was abolished. The academic planning board was to be responsible 'for all aspects of planning – academic, financial, buildings and estates' (Rowe *ibid* a) and was to report to the senate while the vice-chancellor as its chairman presented its recommendations on finance and estates to the finance and general purposes committee 'which would advise Council'. This committee was given delegated powers by council 'to take action on other matters within its terms of reference when it is judged [presumably by the committee itself] that it is urgent, appropriate and in the interests of the university to do so' (Rowe *ibid* b). It could be argued that this was potentially a more dynamic structure than had existed before, designed to speed up decision-making and pull together related decisions of academic planning, finance and physical resources into one set of machinery. On the other hand, it distanced council from critical decision-making, because in effect the finance and general purposes committee could (and did) act on its behalf and, because senior members of the finance and general purposes committee, including the treasurer, were also members of the academic planning board, it reduced the circle of those involved in decision-making. The council had not, in fact, been a particularly effective body and this new structure was intended to ensure that decision-making on critical development issues was not held up by fractious debate.

In parallel with these changes there had been a considerable turnover in the ranks of the senior administrative officers. The structure was for unitary administration headed by a secretary, with a director of finance, a buildings officer and an officer responsible for academic administration, answerable to him. Between 1990 and 1992 the long-standing and respected holders of these last posts all retired and in 1993 the secretary was given early retirement and was replaced by an internal appointee who came from the academic administration side of the house. The pro-vice-chancellors who chaired the two committees of the academic planning board had no particular management experience in the work covered by their committees – the finance director claimed that he had never been asked to provide a cash flow forecast by the budget and monitoring committee (nor indeed by the finance and general purposes committee) and it is clear that the cash flow implications of the actions of the estates committee were not regarded as significant issues. The treasurer, when taking up his appointment in 1992 was asked by the vice-chancellor to be 'a hands off treasurer, not to second guess the director of finance' (Rowe *ibid* c), while according to the report of the Review Committee, the director of finance had been on one occasion criticized at a meeting by the vice-chancellor and by the pro-vice-chancellor, who chaired the estates committee, for circulating a paper at the finance and general purposes committee which set out his concerns about the implications of one capital project and, on a second occasion, had been overruled altogether on the circulation of another paper. The secretary seems to have made no such representations. Although both the director of finance and the director of property services reported notionally to the secretary, the former had a close working relationship with the treasurer and the latter was effectively answerable to the chair of the estates committee.

In effect, the revised governance structure for financial decision-making and capital expenditure was restructured to provide the vice-chancellor with maximum freedom to take action at a time when the administrative/professional chain of command was unstable, and ambiguous, and where professional officers were unable to report their concerns to the bodies charged with making decisions. Such a structure might have coped in normal circumstances, but the vice-chancellor, and the University, which had had virtually no capital development over the last 15 years, having invested heavily in research-active staff for the RAE, were determined to capitalize on the RAE success and improve both the public face of the University and create physical facilities which matched its academic performance. The University found itself committed to four major capital projects: a library extension to which HEFCE had promised £1.4 million subject to the University investing another £4 million and to £400,000 being spent by March 1995, two tranches of new student residences (500 places each and required in October 1995 and October 1996 respectively) costing £7 million each, a rebuilding of the University shopping centre (with residential accommodation provided on the upper floors and new offices for the students' union costing £2.4 million), and a building to house the Ruskin Collection for which the Lottery had promised £2.3 million of £3.1 million overall cost. For each of these projects, planning groups were established by the estates committee but their minutes did not go to the estates committee and eventually there was 'fragmentation of responsibility for each project' (Rowe *ibid* d), and three suffered serious cost overruns with the treasurer acting for the finance and general purposes committee on his own to approve an increase in budget to let one of them go ahead. None appeared to have been approved by the council. Since, for various reasons, all the projects were urgent, and the University lacked the cash to proceed, borrowing had to be envisaged and the University chose to seek a debenture issue. The advice of Barclays de Zoete Wedd Ltd (BZW) was 'that we should aim to be the first [university] in the field of marketing a new style of bond issue' (Rowe *ibid* e). The cost of securing the debenture turned out to be £1 million, but raised £35 million effective from March 1995.

In 1991 Lancaster had external borrowings of under £1 million. By May 1994 this had risen to around £15 million with servicing costs of £2 million, although 65 per cent of these costs were covered from the residential account. The decision to proceed with the bond had to be taken by the council itself. Although the finance and general purposes committee considered several options for generating the required finance, at its meeting in May 1994 council was asked to appoint BZW as the University's professional advisers and in July 1994 to approve the debenture scheme they put forward. The Review rightly criticized the process on these grounds and on the basis of 'The very small number of people in the institution who were fully cognisant of the significance of the action being taken' (Rowe *ibid* f) and of 'The highly experimental nature of the transactions and the lack of precedent, making the University over-dependent on its external advisers' (Rowe *ibid* g). The complexity of the arrangement can be judged by the fact that its meetings in October and December 1994 involved three sets of lawyers to advise members as they came to sign the necessary documents. A further complication was that an 8.5 per cent interest rate could have been achieved in the early summer of 1994 but by September 10 per cent had become the going rate until the HEFCE, under the terms of the Financial Memorandum, intervened to set a maximum rate of 9.75 per cent for approval of the deal and the University had to wait until this rate could be met.

If all this were not enough, two further difficult issues were in play. The first was an early retirement scheme which operated in 1994–95 and 1995–96, primarily to assist with the preparation for the 1995–96 RAE. In the first year (the vice-chancellor's last in office) no sum had been allocated in the budget but the scheme involved expenditure of £1 million. The Premature Retirement Working Party did not meet, business being conducted by correspondence, with failure to respond being taken to signify assent; there was no adequate system for accounting for the costs of the scheme. In the second year, the allocated sum was exceeded by £400,000. The second issue was the merger with the Charlotte Mason College of Education located some 20 miles' distance from the University which had taken place in 1992. No proper due diligence exercise had been undertaken prior to merger and it was only later that deferred maintenance costs and the need for a new library at the College totalling £3 million were calculated. In 1994 the College was incorporated into the University's Faculty of Teacher Education and Training, but in November 1995 an OFSTED inspection gave the English and Mathematics work located in the former College four ratings of unsatisfactory. It rapidly became clear that the costs of reviving the academic performance of the former College together with the capital requirements were, in the situation that the University found itself in the autumn of 1995, impossible to contemplate and the staff and student number base, together with the physical assets, were transferred to the nearby St. Martins College, but not before over £750,000 of redundancy costs and significant administrative costs had been incurred.

At its meeting in July 1995 the council could have reviewed the capital programme and cut back on at least one contract, but the budget for 1995–96 contained an item called 'Reserves' which appears to have been misinterpreted by members and no such decision was taken. During August, however, the vice-chancellor, only months before his retirement, belatedly commissioned a report from KPMG on the University's cash position. As the Review stated:

> It seems incredible to us that the University embarked on a capital building programme of £18.6m ... without carrying out the most careful financial analysis to ensure that at the moment it entered binding contracts to build it could afford to do so in terms both of capital expenditure and cash flow.
>
> (Rowe *ibid* h)

It was soon realized that the University faced a mounting debt profile compounded by the refusal of its bankers to extend borrowing rights unless a recovery plan was embarked upon. According to a Coopers and Lybrand forecast in October 1996 the University would face a cash requirement of £9 million in 1997. Fortunately, with the arrival of a new vice-chancellor and a new secretary, the energy of the University itself, the assistance of HEFCE in re-phasing its recurrent grant payments, an RAE success in 1996, which improved further on that of 1992, and the loss of some 200 posts through a second early retirement scheme, the University was able to restore its ability to meet its debt commitments, although, of course, the long-term repayment of the debenture remained an issue for its successors. The Lancaster case illustrates some basic governance issues:

- The vice-chancellor, and the University as a whole went along with him, was a man in a hurry, and was able to transform the governance and management structures to give himself freedom to engage in a burst of physical development designed to complement the University's research success. There was no independent voice at the governing body level to draw attention to the concentration of decision-making in the hands of a very small group of people or to question the early retirement of the secretary and the lack of proper line management and accountability of the senior management team.

- Under the pressure of business, as described above, all of which had to be conducted to challenging deadlines, governance processes broke down – individual project committees did not send their minutes to the estates committee, chairman's action was used to avoid delays, a premature retirement scheme was launched without provision in the budget and was then conducted in a cavalier fashion without proper accountability or record-keeping, no proper due diligence exercise, whether academic or financial was carried out prior to the merger with Charlotte Mason College. What the Review describes as a 'can do – must do' culture took over and obscured good governance and management practice.

- The governing body allowed itself to be marginalized by an unwise, unfettered delegation of power to its finance and general purposes committee, which itself allowed its chair to act on its behalf. In two critical issues, the decision to seek a debenture and the approval of the 1995–96 budget, with its implications for proceeding with the full range of items in the capital programme, the council allowed itself to be under-informed and was altogether too passive in its response to material put to it. By the same token, the council was ill served by its secretary and professional officers in allowing this to take place. What amounted to the muzzling of the director of finance by the vice-chancellor and pro-vice- chancellor should have been challenged. In the end, however, because of the requirements of the bond issue the council had to take corporate and individual responsibility for decisions, which, in effect, had been taken in its name.

- The question needs to be asked as to where the audit committee was while this expenditure was taking place. The role of the external auditors and the audit committee should have been to scrutinize the accounts and the financial forecasts to establish whether the capital programme was sustainable in the light of the University's other commitments. It should certainly have called for an independent assessment of the BZW proposed debenture. Only when the outgoing vice-chancellor commissioned a report from KPMG in August 1995 did the audit committee enter the scene and then it imposed a confidentiality restriction on its report so that it could not be considered by the senate. The inaction of the audit committee again denied the council the independent opinion it should have received on the University's financial affairs.

- Even though this was a university with a 'civic university' constitution, the senate's role in the capital programme embarked upon was minimal. The academic planning board was formally required to report to the senate but in fact it did not do so in a comprehensive manner and most information appears to have been given orally under 'vice-chancellor's business'. The senate had itself accepted the merger with Charlotte Mason College uncritically and had not undertaken its assessment of the academic weaknesses of the College with sufficient rigour. But nevertheless the strategic issues, academic, financial and physical, should have been discussed by the senate and the Review was right to recommend that 'all strategic issues to be decided by the Council are first brought to the Senate' (Rowe *ibid* i).

- The above recommendation, however, highlights the heart of the problem because the governance structure made no adequate provision for the consideration of strategy. The fundamental strategic issue for the University was that it had invested heavily in RAE success to the exclusion of its capital infrastructure. This may or may not have been in the circumstances a sensible strategy but it should have been entered into knowingly. It then embarked on a programme to overcome the shortcomings of the previous strategy without appreciating the extent to which the commitments of its previous strategy had imposed resource constraints on its freedom of action. Prior to 1993 the University had no formal machinery for considering strategy, although the finance committee might have been expected to consider longer range finance issues and the academic planning committee academic issues, but the council and the senate were entitled to expect that this kind of strategic appraisal might have emerged from the new academic planning board but in fact this proved to be a vehicle for 'doing' rather than strategy, in spite of its terms of reference. As a result, council had no strategic framework within which to consider the bond issue and had not discussed at all whether the urgency for action proposed by the vice-chancellor through the academic planning board was consistent with the University's forecast financial position.

Sources: The primary source is Rowe, P. (ed.) (1997) *The University of Lancaster, Review of Institutional Lessons to be Learned 1994–1996*, University of Lancaster. Also drawn on: McClintoch, M. and Ritchie, W. (2003) 'Capital building and cash flow at the University of Lancaster' in Warner, D. and Palfreyman, D. (eds) (2003) *Managing Crisis*, Maidenhead: Open University Press; National Audit Office (1998) *The Management of Building Projects at English Higher Education Institutions*, HC 452 Session 1997–98, HMSO; personal knowledge of the author.

The University of Cambridge

The Cambridge case relates to the breakdown in governance and management associated with the Capsa disaster where a new information technology (IT) management system was installed without adequate preparation, and at considerable unanticipated costs, which brought the financial management of the University to a virtual standstill for a short while and which stimulated widespread calls for an inquiry into what had gone wrong. Unlike the Cardiff and Lancaster cases, however, the financial viability of the University was never for a moment in question – the level of Cambridge's reserves were certainly such as to contain a £10 million overspend on an IT system that did not work – but the issues the Capsa affair raised for the governance of the University had a wider relevance beyond the rather idiosyncratic governance structure of Cambridge itself.

The Cambridge governing structure comprised a council and the Regent House, both bodies, at the time of the Capsa troubles, themselves riven with internal disagreements, together with a general board of the faculties which dealt with academic and educational affairs. The council was chaired by the vice-chancellor (thus contravening a central tenet of the Cadbury Report that the post of chairman of the board should be separated from that of chief executive) and had 'general responsibility for the administration of the University . . . and of the management of its resources' and the power 'to take such actions as are necessary for it to discharge those responsibilities' (Statute A, Chapter IV para. 1(b)). The Regent House comprised the academic staff of the University and was the formal governing body of the University with power to overrule the council. As a consequence, and in the interests of running the University effectively, the council had arrived at processes, such as creating administrative posts on a temporary three-year basis, which avoided scrutiny by the Regent House, but which also raised the level of distrust of the Regent House in the council. It also created instability amongst the staff appointed and probably ensured that the most effective staff were not secured. The council had resisted acknowledging that the vice-chancellor was chief executive of the University, although he was universally accepted as the University's academic leader, and the registrary, the notional head of the administration, was not statutorily answerable to him, but to the council, although in practice the relationship had much of the traditional vice- chancellor–registrar relationship about it. In 1989 the Wass Committee in its *Report of the Syndicate appointed to consider the Government of the University* had recommended that the administration of the University be unified under the registrary, but 11 years later under the statutes, neither the secretary general of the faculties nor the treasurer (unlike Lancaster and Cardiff a full-time administrative post), was formally answerable to the registrary, the treasurer remaining under the statutes as the council's principal adviser on the University's assets and investments reporting direct to the vice-chancellor. In 1999 the University had created the post of director of finance but the reporting arrangements of the post, whether direct to the registrary or to the treasurer, were unclear and ambiguous, and were a cause of significant tension to the person appointed to the post, especially in relation to overall financial management and the management of the University's significant investment portfolio.

The council had two committees that dealt with finance, the finance committee and the planning and resources committee, both of which had a role in the Capsa disaster. The finance committee approved Oracle as the preferred supplier and established the target date for implementation as being 1 August 2000, but the planning and resources committee, on the basis of a wholly fallacious cost benefit analysis, approved the expenditure of the necessary resources to fund the project and appointed the first project manager. Since no funds had been included in the University's budget it was agreed that the sum should be withdrawn from a capital fund and that a sinking fund should be established to replenish the fund over 10 years. No sinking fund was ever established. Meantime the principal officers (that is the registrary, the treasurer and the secretary general of the faculties) appointed a steering committee for the project whose minutes went to the finance committee. This steering committee, however, was not charged to manage the project which, although begun under the treasurer, moved to a new appointee, the director of management information services, who reported to the registrary; in practice, the project was driven by the director of finance. In effect, no one and no body could be described as being managerially in charge. The council, the finance committee, the planning and resources committee and the Regent House must share responsibility for starving the administration of adequate resources, particularly in the finance/IT area, to do the job that was required of it: Cambridge was proud of the fact that it spent approximately half the percentage of its budget on administration that other UK research-intensive universities did (and it showed).

This confusion was matched by the presence of two separate watchdog committees, the audit committee and the board of scrutiny. The former operated broadly as a traditional university audit committee except that its chair and a majority of its members were internal to the University; the latter had been created on the recommendation of the Wass Committee and had a roving commission to inquire into any matter, academic as well as financial, in the University; its membership was entirely academic, by election, and, unlike the audit committee's, its reports were often controversial within the council. In the case of Capsa it advised the University in every year from 1996 that the operation was inadequately resourced. The audit committee and the council were served by external and internal auditors. An internal audit service was established in 1993 with the appointment of an experienced internal auditor. Having commented repeatedly on the lack of management information systems and an appropriate resourcing commitment the internal auditor commented adversely on the planning and resources committee's decision to set 1 August 2000 as the implementation date and in her report to the audit committee was unable to give the committee an assurance that the University's financial systems were sound because of 'entrenched weaknesses in management information systems and research grants administration' (quoted in Shattock 2001 a). Both sets of comments were ignored, although under audit practice the report would have had to go to the vice-chancellor and to the council, as well as to the audit committee itself. Unsurprisingly, the internal auditor resigned to go to another job and was replaced by Robson Rhodes. In June 2000 Robson Rhodes wrote a critical report to the audit committee about the decision to go live on 1 August and the need for a contingency plan. The report was never seen by the Capsa steering committee and the audit committee decided that any delay would lead to loss of momentum. At the same time the external auditors in their Management Letters raised issues about the need to examine a 'business' strategy before drawing up an IT strategy and to review governance structures to ensure that centrally agreed IT policy decisions were not vitiated by the development of bespoke systems in departments. The Management Response to these points was to fail to produce either a business or an IT strategy and to reply to the second point that it recognized the 'underlying dichotomy in the University's management and administrative system, that of the role of the centre *vis à vis* relatively autonomous departments' but that while external processes (such as the HEFCE Audit Code) and 'the demands of efficiency and value for money' might indicate the need for more unified controls 'the culture of the University remains in favour of a dissipation of power and authority. Until this essential conundrum has been resolved and a new paradigm established it is difficult to see how more than modest progress can be made' (quoted in Shattock 2001 *ibid* b). In other words: the University accepted the external auditor's verdict but was unable to implement it. The audit committee was fully apprised of the adverse criticisms of the Capsa programme, as voiced by both external and internal auditors, as were the principal officers, but chose not to make statements that would make uncomfortable reading at the finance or planning and resources committees and did not give sufficient warnings to the council. It did not provide the independent view that the University required.

The result was that when the new system went live on 1 August 2000 it failed immediately; departments had not prepared for the changeover and were not staffed up for a new and demanding system; an understaffed central finance office was unable to cope with the turmoil; and a system which had initially been allocated £377,000 in 1996 had escalated to costing over £10 million and rising. More important than the financial loss the affair was rightly seen as a symptom of wider governance and management failings in the University.

The Cambridge case illustrates the following basic issues:

• The danger of an internal culture whose self-belief is so strong that it rejects external comment and criticism. The value of internal and external audit processes is that they should provide a dispassionate commentary on an institution's management of its financial affairs. The internal auditor had, in effect, qualified the University's accounts and her report was discounted by the audit committee and the University's senior management. Subsequent internal audit and external audit reports were not acted upon. The audit committee, the majority of whose membership was made up of internal staff, did not reflect the depth and importance of these issues to the council.

• There was ambiguity in the governance structure of which committee was responsible for key decision-making over the Capsa project. Reports and minutes were circulated (or not circulated) to the several bodies but there was no direct line of accountability except that statutorily laid on the council itself. A similar ambiguity occurred in relation to managerial responsibility and accountability. Cambridge did not have the unified administration which had been accepted in principle more than 10 years previously, and authority and reporting lines were muddled and confused.

• Issues of governance and authority between the council and the academic departments remained unresolved and as a consequence coherent action was absent and the implementation of policy deriving from the central decision-making bodies was weak.

• The University underestimated the importance of employing sufficient professional staff to carry out the functions imposed upon them. The administration was seriously under-funded and administrative staff were not accorded the respect and status that their importance to the running of the University deserved. At best they were seen as a 'necessary evil' rather than as partners in a common enterprise.

Sources: Shattock, M.L. (2001) 'Review of university management and governance arising out of the Capsa project', Report to the Audit Committee and the Board of Scrutiny, *Cambridge University Reporter*, Vol. CXXX II No. 6, 2 November; personal knowledge of the author.

Troubles over chief executives

The University of Huddersfield

The University of Huddersfield is a post-1992 HEC and the events described below occurred within two years of its translation to university status. Like Cardiff, however, the Huddersfield difficulties, followed quickly by those at Portsmouth, had an important impact on the discussion of governance issues in higher education. Most notably they prompted the first publication of the CUC's *Guide* and the publicity they attracted led to the governance of higher education being examined by the Nolan Committee on Standards in Public Life. One aspect of the difficulties at Huddersfield, the severance package accorded to its vice-chancellor, became the subject of an NAO report (NAO 1995) and of a hearing by the Public Accounts Committee.

Like all HECs, Huddersfield had a governing body, which itself formed the legal corporation, and an academic board. In 1994 the director of the polytechnic/vice-chancellor of the University had been in post for 24 years and was known for his 'forceful personality and style of management' (Committee of Public Accounts 1995). Huddersfield was a strongly local and regional institution rooted in the activities and industries of its region. As a polytechnic it had resisted a potential merger with a neighbouring university and it had clashed with its local authority in the early 1980s over funding levels, a case that the Council for National Academic Awards had supported in one of its regular institutional reviews. The director ran the polytechnic through his governing body without much involvement of his academic board. Several members of the governing body had been awarded honorary degrees by the governing body while remaining sitting members.

An HEC governing body is restricted to between 12 and 24 members and carries the expectation that this membership will contain two academic staff representatives and one student. The vice-chancellor persuaded the governing body to opt for the smallest possible membership, quoting company board analogies, with the intention of eliminating the need for a traditional committee structure, except for an audit and a remuneration committee. In reducing the membership to only 12 the decision was taken under Schedule 6 of the legislation to exclude staff and student representation that had existed on the governing body of the former polytechnic, on the excuse that they were representatives and answerable to local constituencies and therefore were not able to exercise a proper independence as members. Long-standing internal discontent then erupted in demonstrations by staff organizations and by students. These culminated in a referendum of all staff and students by the joint union council, a liaison body between trade unions representing staff and students, in which 98 per cent of those voting (61 per cent of those balloted) expressed no confidence in the governing body. It was clear that the focus of the discontent was the vice-chancellor and he was persuaded by the governors to resign subject to appropriate severance terms. The governing body then advertised the post of vice-chancellor at a salary of £120,000, approximately 25 per cent higher than the average vice-chancellorial salary at the time on the grounds that it wished to attract a high-quality appointee who would attract other high-quality staff.

If this salary caused surprise it was not as much as was shown for the severance package offered the sitting vice-chancellor by the governing body. The vice-chancellor was, at the time, 65 years old, but was on a four-year contract awarded when he was 63 that took him to age 67. First, his salary was raised to the advertised level of his successor and back-dated from the end of July to 1 February 1994 (this represented a 40 per cent salary increase). This gave him a lump sum of £211,000 to which was added a further compensatory sum of £200,000, cover for him and his family from BUPA and retention of a car until July 1996. The scandal that this provoked when revealed in the media persuaded HEFCE to take legal advice on the basis of which the chief executive of HEFCE decided that there was a *prima facia* case that the payment constituted a misuse of public funds, the reasons for it were 'insufficient and flawed' and the arrangements made 'were so irrational and excessive' as to be *ultra vires* (NAO 1995 a). The governing body was given five days to withdraw the offer. A new severance package amounting to no more than £150,000 was offered effective from January 1995 when the vice-chancellor's contract was terminated.

With effect from October 1994 Sir William Taylor was drafted in to be acting vice-chancellor, the governing body was expanded, and staff and student members restored, and a new internal governance structure was established more along the lines of a civic university than a traditional HEC. In 2000 the Huddersfield governing body indicated to CUC that were it not for the legal requirements of the 1992 Act it would seek to expand its membership beyond the figure of 24 to which HECs were limited. The CUC's reaction to the exclusion of staff and student representatives, mindful of the wording of the 1992 Act which did not make their membership a legal requirement for HECs, was to issue advice (NAO 1995 Appendix 5), subsequently recorded in the *Guide*, that if any governing body in the future was to consider their removal it should minute carefully the reasons why such action was taken and publish it within the institution so as to make the decision both transparent and open to challenge. This has proved to be a sufficient deterrent to any other university seeking to follow Huddersfield's lead, should that have been necessary.

Huddersfield's case is in a way so flagrant that it seems almost anomalous to highlight particular issues:

- The first must be that however one reads the case the vice-chancellor and the members of the reduced governing body were too close to one another for the members to be in a position to make independent judgements about his remuneration. The fact that several had been awarded honours by a governing body on which they continued to sit raised important questions about their independence.
- The case for the decision to reduce the governing body to a unitary board of 12 was flawed because, as is argued above, the analogy with company boards is unsound and, in this case, rendered the governing body open to the criticism of cronyism and to being

subservient to an over-dominant vice-chancellor. The removal of staff and student members might, under this interpretation, have been motivated simply by a wish to eliminate dissentient voices rather than because of any concern about conflicts of interest.

• One has to ask about the role of the secretary of the governing body. Did the secretary advise against the determination to exclude the staff and student members? Legal advice it was said was sought by the governing body before the offer of a severance package was made to the vice-chancellor. Was that advice sought via the secretary or direct by one of the members? In any event it seemed to be flawed if the legal advice taken by HEFCE was regarded as sufficient to justify the HEFCE Chief Executive's instruction to withdraw the initial package.

• The Huddersfield affair came to light as a public issue because staff and students not only held a referendum on the performance of the governing body which was picked up by the media, but also because they communicated with their local MP who took up their case. But the roots of this situation lay in the gulf that existed between the governing body and the academic board and the inability of the latter body to exercise any influence on the decisions of the former. One of the immediate actions of the acting vice-chancellor was to set up joint committees between the governing body and the academic board as well as reinvigorating the academic board itself.

• HEFCE's action to force the withdrawal of the original severance package represented not only a severe corrective to a maverick governing body but an example of the exercise of HEFCE's powers, as conferred by the Financial Memorandum; these were not available to the UGC at the time of the Cardiff affair. Institutional autonomy was now subject to qualification when questions of public accountability were at issue.

Sources: Committee of Public Accounts (1995) *Severence Payments to Senior Staff in the Publicly Funded Education Sector*, Minutes of Evidence, Monday 20 February 1995, London: HMSO; National Audit Office Report by the Comptroller and Auditor General (1995) *Severance Payments to Senior Staff in the Publicly Funded Education Sector*, London: HMSO; personal knowledge of the author.

The University of Portsmouth

Portsmouth, like Huddersfield, is a post-1992 HEC and had been one of the most highly regarded polytechnics with a solid research reputation. But on the death of its respected president (polytechnic director) in office in 1990 there had been difficulties within the governing body processes about his replacement. One recruitment process had been aborted when the vice-president (business and finance), who had been a senior academic in a pre-1992 university, had been recommended for appointment but a change of heart at governing body level had led to the post not being filled. The recruitment process was restarted and the vice-president became acting president for a year between August 1990 to August 1991. In June 1991 a new president was appointed from outside the polytechnic and the acting president became deputy president keeping, however, his portfolio of business and finance. But in June 1994, after an organizational review conducted by the vice-chancellor, the chair of the governing body decided that the deputy vice-chancellor (as he had now become following changes of title after the award of university status) should be replaced by a new professional appointment of director of finance, and his other duties distributed amongst the pro-vice-chancellors and that his post would, therefore, become redundant. The governing body, however, was not asked to consider the question of the restructuring of the directorate as a matter of principle until October 1994 after the redundancy, which was intrinsic to the re-structuring, had been declared and after the deputy vice-chancellor had signed a compromise agreement in respect to a severance package.

This was not the only problem, however, to beset the University. In the autumn of 1993 the finance officer approached his line manager the deputy vice-chancellor (business and finance) with evidence of possible financial irregularities on the vice-chancellor's part in respect to travel claims. The deputy vice-chancellor reported this evidence to the chair of the audit committee who, having consulted the chair of governors commissioned the internal auditors, an external firm of accountants, to conduct a preliminary investigation. In November the chair of governors, the deputy chair of governors and the chair of the audit committee issued a formal reprimand to the vice-chancellor, but the chair of the audit committee asked the internal auditors to carry out a wider investigation to satisfy the audit committee that there were no further discrepancies. In March 1994 the internal auditors reported back to the audit committee but at a meeting of the committee also attended by the chair of governors it was decided that the reprimand already issued was an appropriate response to the findings and that the matter should end there. HEFCE was informed as to the outcome as required under the terms of the Financial Memorandum. However, the internal auditor's full report was not shown to the original complainants (which meant that they had no opportunity to comment on the detail of the material on which, bearing in mind their positions, they were well qualified to do) but only the recommendations and was not made available to members of the governing body as required under a procedural circular on the investigation of alleged financial irregularities applying to staff generally that had been issued to the University on the authority of the audit committee the previous year.

Subsequently, further revelations appeared in the media and strong protest votes were recorded by the staff of the University. Following a special meeting of the governing body to consider the widened allegations the vice-chancellor resigned.

The Portsmouth case raised extraordinarily difficult issues and it is clear that in trying to deal with them the members of the governing body who were involved sought to act throughout in the best interests of the University. They were, however, confronted with procedural issues of great complexity. Although there had been allegations of impropriety made against vice-chancellors in the past the only clear case occurred in a pre-1992 institution with a very different constitution some years previously and had in any case been resolved by the head of the institution resigning, so there were no precedents to follow, even if the Portsmouth governors had sought to do so. A further consideration was that these events took place shortly after the translation to university status and the governors were perhaps particularly aware of the potential public damage that could be done to the institution by the tarnishing of its reputation. In practice, of course, the inappropriate conduct of the vice-chancellor did become public and the concern of the staff ensured that, in the short term at least, the University did suffer damage to its reputation. At various points the case illustrates where issues of judgement can come up against matters of procedure and constitution, and where damage can be caused by embarking on actions for managerial reasons that conflict with questions of constitutional integrity:

- Whatever the arguments there might have been for a structural reorganization and bringing in greater professionalism in the leadership of the finance area (and there were many other ways in which this could have been approached if this was indeed judged to be necessary), to proceed to declare the deputy vice-chancellor redundant before a discussion of the structural issues at the governing body and at a time when he was involved in forwarding an allegation against the vice-chancellor's conduct, would seem to have been a serious error of judgement. Quite apart from the important procedural issues, and the background in relation to the recruitment of the vice-chancellor, the potential entanglement of the two issues and the burden on the decision-makers was such that they should have been kept completely separate in time as well as in procedure.

- Because of concern about reputational issues – both the institution's and, no doubt, the vice-chancellor's – senior members of the governing body and the audit committee acted as if they had delegated powers when they did not and did not fully involve the governing body. With hindsight this was unwise. It was by no means clear that the chair of governors, the deputy chair and the chair of the audit committee or the audit committee had the power to issue a reprimand or confirm one. A governing body is entitled to know if its chief executive is guilty of inappropriate conduct especially when under the Financial Memorandum he is the responsible officer for the financial integrity of the institution. The governing body did, of course, establish an independent inquiry in February 1995, which reported fully on the critical issues in September, and which brought matters to a head.

- The case underlines the importance of the audit process in modern university governance and of the value in certain circumstances of an internal audit team which is entirely external to the institution.

- While the senior lay officers' concern for reputational issues is understandable they appear to have undervalued the moral authority a vice-chancellor must have in dealing with institutional issues. Even if the affair had not become public after the initial reprimand, the finance officer, the deputy vice-chancellor and at least some others working in the centre of the University were aware of what had taken place. It is most unlikely, in the circumstances, that trust would have been restored. The senior lay officers acted too hastily in issuing their initial reprimand and would have been better advised to await the results of the full investigation, but in any case, once a *prima facia* case of this kind had been established the vice-chancellor's effectiveness in office would always have been in doubt and his position compromised. This was emphasized by the reaction of staff to the situation as it developed in the media.

Sources: Committee of Public Accounts (1995) *Severance Payments to Senior Staff in the Publicly Funded Education Sector*, Minutes of Evidence, Monday 20 February 1998, London: HMSO; National Audit Office (1995) *Severance Payments to Senior Staff in the Publicly Funded Education Sector*, London: HMSO; personal knowledge of the author.

The Southampton Institute of Higher Education

This case reflects the problems of unbridled ambition in an environment where market-driven expansion was officially encouraged, without an appropriate framework of governance capable of putting a check on the executive. The Institute had been formed in 1984 by the merger of two colleges, the Southampton Colleges of Art and of Technology, and in 1986 the College of Nautical Studies was added. Until 1989 the Institute was the responsibility of the Hampshire County Council which had restricted its higher education development in order to concentrate growth at the Portsmouth Polytechnic (later the University of Portsmouth). With the Institute's incorporation and legal independence from its local authority following the Education Reform Act, and the appointment of a new director who 'made no secret of his intention to develop the institute on commercial lines as an entrepreneurial institution' (Brown 2003 a), constraints were removed and a period of very rapid expansion occurred in parallel with the sudden surge in applications in that year across the whole of higher education. Even though this was brought to an end in 1993–94, the Institute had doubled its student numbers in this period to over 10,000. During the 1988–93 period the Institute had tried and failed to gain polytechnic status and to achieve accreditation from the National Council for Academic Awards. It was later (1995) to fail to gain degree-awarding status through the Higher Education Quality Council (HEQC). Its degrees had therefore to be validated by another institution (Nottingham Trent University).

At incorporation the new HEC had a board of 19 members and five committees, including audit, governance, remuneration and resources. But the board, which met only four times a year, was dominated by a small group, the chair, vice-chair and the director who all sat on the five-person governance and remuneration committees and on the resources committee which had eight members (one of whom told the HEFCE Auditors that he had 'no relevant knowledge or expertise' (NAO 1998)) which dealt with all aspects of finance and estates business. This body met, on a scheduled basis, only three times a year, but was given delegated powers of decision-taking by the governing body in crucial areas, such as opening a campus in Athens, and on major capital programmes. In practice, much of the day-to-day handling of issues relating to the committee seems to have been carried through by the chair, vice-chair and the director together with the director of resources and the director of academic affairs (the last two being professional officers reporting to the director). In 1992, a new academic organization was adopted with the grouping of divisions into three schools under directors who held permanent appointments and reported to the Institute director. Two years later this structure was changed so that the three school directors took on cross-Institute roles, and the divisions became nine faculties headed by deans. A year later the director announced, without consultation, a further restructuring under which the nine faculties were to become six. This, according to Brown, became 'the catalyst for the crisis' (Brown *ibid* b). None of these reorganizations appears to have been discussed at the governing body level but ordained by the director. Indeed the management style of the director became increasingly unpopular on the campus and over the period 1995–97 staff took their grievances to HEFCE, the Campaign for Academic Freedom and the press. (Grievance procedures within the Institute culminated in a final decision by the director even when he was the subject of the grievance.) From a governance point of view matters went from bad to worse when the director for corporate development, the secretary of the governing body, was given voluntary severance, it being widely believed as a direct result of his having led a deputation to the chair of governors to express the view that the directors had lost confidence in the head of the institution. The post was not replaced and the director of resources took over the secretaryship of the audit committee (and of the governing body) in direct contravention of good governance practice. Votes of no confidence were subsequently passed by staff and students.

The Southampton Institute case, however, threw up some novel features. The first relates to the role of the resources committee and close partnership of the chair, vice-chair and director. One result of the close down of home student number expansion in 1993–94 by HEFCE was the stimulus it gave to the Institute for overseas ventures, mostly through franchising arrangements, and in March 1995 its corporate strategy document, approved by the governing body, included an aim to generate a surplus of 10 per cent in turnover, after payment of overheads, on such operations. Eight such enterprises were set up with private colleges of unremarkable academic quality in Greece, Ireland, Spain and India. All of them were failures: in one case the college closed, in another no students were recruited. In two cases there were large losses. The first related to the establishment of an Institute presence in Athens, apparently located in a 'red light district', under the auspices of a private company formed by the Institute, and the second was a project set up just as the Athens campus was being closed (at a loss of some £600,000) to offer joint degrees and short courses with a Spanish maritime institution (from which it decided to withdraw in 1997 at a loss of some £300,000).

The resources committee had delegated responsibility for the financial side of these ventures but appears to have had no strategy framework within which they considered them and no evaluation procedure. In 1996, the director took legal advice to establish whether a HEQC report, which severely criticized the Athens venture on quality grounds, could be suppressed.

Individual complaints to HEFCE over a range of issues, including the financial arrangements for the Athens venture, prompted HEFCE auditors to visit the Institute and compile three separate reports, in November 1996 and two in October 1997. The memorandum eventually submitted to HEFCE in 1998 was published as an appendix in the NAO report (NAO 1998). As part of its examination of governance issues the HEFCE auditors discussed management information issues and board procedures with members of the governing body. The responses illustrated only too clearly the breakdown of trust between some members and the inner circle described above. Twelve members out of 19 were dissatisfied with information received on the Institute's overseas operations, including that management only began releasing information about Athens when the project started to go wrong, and that the 'adverse position' on the Spanish venture was not known officially by the board. Some members commented on 'too much information', 'misleading' information or information that had been 'massaged' or was 'very complex'. Thirteen expressed concern at their inability to make a contribution to key debates – the board atmosphere was 'daunting', their contributions were 'pushed aside', 'decisions were unclear', 'there isn't a chair, there's a triumvirate', 'meetings are a shambles', 'there is intimidation', 'there is no proper debate', 'some members appear inhibited' (NAO 1998 b). Many board members 'felt that they had not discharged their responsibilities because of their own uncertainty and lack of cohesiveness' (NAO 1998 c). The HEFCE auditors' first report was not sent to the audit committee.

In 1996 after the votes of no confidence the governing body commissioned the retired director of Brighton polytechnic to carry out a communications audit. His report, delivered in November 1996, was highly critical of the director's management style, frequent reorganizations and the climate of fear which prevented staff from speaking out on institutional issues. The report was adopted at the board's meeting in December 1996 and challenged by the director at a meeting of the board in January 1997 on the grounds that the governing body had 'exceeded their powers', because it overrode his responsibilities under the Articles of Government for 'the organisation, direction and management of the Institute and the leadership of its staff' (NAO 1995 d). The director took legal advice on the paper he presented to the Board and this raised a fundamental issue as to whether such action constituted an appropriate expenditure, as it was clearly self-interested. (The CUC *Guide* now makes it clear that such advice should only be sought on behalf of the governing body itself by the secretary to the governing body.) To complete the picture, the director also hired an ex-police chief superintendent to investigate and identify the authors of a samizdat publication, *Dunghill* circulated electronically which satirized the Institute's own official internal journal, *Molehill*. Insufficient evidence was found and no action was taken.

In November 1997 the director resigned, and an acting director was appointed. The chair and the vice-chair also left office, as did the chair of the audit committee.

The Southampton case raises some particular issues.

• The danger of a powerful clique of governors and a chief executive dominating a governing body. Such a clique can not only exclude other members from the participation in decision-making for which they are legally responsible but can also be inefficient. The resources committee was not challenged on its management of the Institute's overseas operations; had it been some of its worst decisions might have been rectified more quickly. The responses from governors to the HEFCE auditors' questions reveal a breakdown of effectiveness within the board that completely vitiated its role as a governing body.

• The delegation of such far-reaching powers to the resources committee both reinforced the situation and deprived the board of its ability to exercise appropriate control over entrepreneurial activity. The audit committee, which could have been a check on the resources committee, seems to have exercised no influence over events. In the circumstances of the time and in the light of the corporate strategy approved by the board some risks were inevitable, but the board seems to have taken no steps to evaluate whether the Institute management was confronting these risks with professional competence. In particular, the board seems never to have debated the frequent administrative and academic reorganizations which proved to be so destructive of staff morale.

• The board had no policy for succession planning for its own membership. Both the chair and the vice-chair were 70 and had been in office for a substantial period – the chair since 1984. One member had apparently served for 27 years. It was wholly dependent on the drive and autocratic direction of the director and lacked any independence of decision-making until the weight of adverse external and internal comment led to the appointment of an outsider to look at communication within the Institute. This eventually provoked an unprecedented confrontation with the director which it was inevitable he would lose.

Sources: Brown, R. (2003) 'Southampton Institute' in Warner, D. and Palfreyman, D. (eds) (2003) *Managing Crisis*, Maidenhead: Open University Press; NAO (1998) *Overseas operations, Governance and Management at Southampton Institute*, HC 23 Session 1998–90, London: The Stationery Office, 11 December; personal knowledge of the author.

Academic governance ∎

By their nature internal problems of academic governance carry a less high profile than the cases described above because they do not obviously threaten the viability of the institution and, for this reason, they do not attract the attention of the media. Yet such problems do impact on the integrity of central organs of the University's governance and institutions' governance processes and can have a serious effect on the level of academic performance. Sometimes, as in the Southampton Institute where autocratically directed academic reorganizations alienated the academic community, academic governance issues can play a fundamental role in provoking wider institutional crisis but, in themselves, they rarely provide the basis for external inquiry.

The cases described below were part of institutional attempts to adjust their structures to changing environments and represent the best efforts of institutional leaders and others to adapt existing governance arrangements to new circumstances. These circumstances have been described above and may be summarized here as institutional size and manageability, the development of a more marketized higher education system that demanded quicker response times, a view across public sector organizations as a whole that in periods of financial stringency decisions about resources need to be devolved from the centre to closer to the point of action and a sometimes contradictory recognition that, for strategic reasons, academic, financial and physical resource issues needed to be brought together in the centre for effective decision-making. By far the most important impact of these changes on academic governance has been in the way central academic decision-making is co-ordinated with the interests of the academic heartland of departments, disciplines and the actual teaching and research processes. A vice-chancellor writing in 1966 in a multi-faculty civic university of no more than 5000 students could condemn the idea of making deanships full time as representing a 'smaller and more authoritarian oligarchy' which would reduce the size and complexity of the committee structure but would be unacceptable because 'academic freedom would be restricted and academics would carry out research and teaching less well. The academic does not produce best performance to order' (Aitken 1966). In the modern university the role of dean, however, has become a key element in academic governance and the cases described below illustrate different approaches to the need to provide a bridge between the central academic authorities and the basic units.

University A

University A is an Australian 'sandstone' university, that is, the equivalent of a UK old civic university, with a distinguished research record and a very strong market position within the Australian higher education system for student recruitment. It is not surprising that the concept of 'executive deans' within an Anglo-Saxon governance model originated in Australia because Australia faced the onset of market forces following the Dawkins reforms in 1988 before their impact was felt anything like as strongly in the UK. University A had decided, with the consent of its senate and in common with many other Australian universities, that elected deans, or deans appointed by the vice-chancellor from within the university, were no longer meeting the needs of a university whose funding was formula based from the state and market based in relation to overseas student fees and research income. It wanted to devolve budgets and market sensitivity to the faculties in the expectation that this would encourage initiatives at the grass roots academic level, leaving the centre with a steering, regulatory and corporate accountability role. It was convinced that for faculties to fulfill this role they had to be well led by deans who had high academic standing and managerial skills. It seemed logical therefore to advertise the posts worldwide in order to find the best candidates. The posts were given a five-year tenure, although there was an expectation that the holders would be absorbed into the relevant academic departments at the end of that time if not continued as deans. In the end, one internal appointment was made and the rest were from outside the university, one from the US. The university made good appointments – all the appointees had strong academic records and experience of management at the level of department headships.

The appointments did not, however, work. The centre regarded the new deans as competing with one another for resources, on behalf of their faculties, and therefore held them at arms' length; the faculties felt that they were part of central management because, inevitably, they pressed what seemed like the university's case for rationalization and income generation. Moreover, the centre made the dean's salaries, and those of their offices, a faculty charge so that the costs fell onto the faculty budgets. The deans, as academics, wanted to maintain their own research and to engage in teaching, not least to integrate themselves into their faculties' academic life. Research was difficult because start-up funds were not available except from the faculty budget, and where laboratories were involved, it meant obtaining bench space in academic departments that were tightly controlled through a charge out scheme for space. Teaching was even more problematic because in addition to finding regular slots in the dean's diary, the insertion of the dean into a department's teaching timetable reduced a department's case for increased resources for teaching. With the reluctance of departments to seek to engage with the new deans in an academic sense, the prospect of absorption into a department at the end of a five-year deanship looked much less likely. The deans were, therefore, neither fish nor fowl – they were regarded as predators by the centre because they competed for additional resources and as imposed outsiders by the faculties brought in to match central priorities, which they were required to pay for.

In their working lives there were also difficulties. Whilst they were budget holders for their faculties they were chairs of faculty committees which could take different views to them on resource allocation issues. As 'executive' deans they could impose their decisions, but to make a practice of doing so was to reduce the opportunity of developing a consensus about priorities.

After several deans had resigned the university decided to move back to internal appointments while retaining the executive dean title.

University B

University B is a major South African university whose governance structure is strongly aligned with the UK civic university model. In the post-apartheid era it was anxious to regain the 'world-class' status it believed it had held in the past and it determined to reorganize to face the challenge of the future. One of these was that, although it was receiving level funding from the State, in parts of the university student numbers were falling and in parts they were rising. During the period of apartheid its antipathy to racism had justified the maintenance of a strongly consensual, participative form of governance as a way of withstanding the pressures on it exerted both by the State and by society in general. The university had an overlarge, unreformed senate and a senate general purposes committee which was much too large to act in a 'steering' capacity. As a consequence the vice-chancellor used an executive management meeting (which did not include the deans) for getting things done but had also created an extended executive management meeting which did include the deans. These two bodies tended to pass business from one to the other, both trivial and policy orientated; neither communicated effectively with the statutory bodies. It was felt that the university structure was subject to considerable inertia and that more dynamism was needed.

A first step for reform was to dissolve the unitary administration under a highly respected registrar to create a tertiary structure with a director of financial services and a director of development both reporting direct to the vice-chancellor. This did not work well, and the director of financial services, brought in from the private sector, embarked on a new financial accounting system that proved to be expensive and inefficient, leading to her departure. More important from a governance point of view was that the vice-chancellor, impressed by the rhetoric from Australia about the effectiveness of executive deans, decided to follow suit, and seven new executive deans were appointed, mostly from within the university. Unfortunately, although the senate and council had been persuaded to follow this route to reform, no attempt had been made to revise the University's internal legislation. This particularly caused conflict with the position of head of department where the regulations made clear that heads of departments were answerable to the council, through the faculty board and the senate, with no reference whatever to deans. Moreover, while deans could disassociate themselves from decisions of their faculty boards, they could not stand in the way of those decisions being submitted as resolutions or recommendations to the senate. This became an important issue because in two faculties falling student numbers raised questions about the viability of the academic departmental structures, a situation which, at one level, might seem to justify the role of an executive dean. However, the executive dean lacked powers to resolve the problems and in one case a dean, having had his proposals for departmental mergers voted down by his faculty board, joined with the faculty board in resisting pressure from the centre to proceed with them.

In two other areas there were difficulties in the reform process. The previous period of the university's history had been politically troublesome and the university had built up a formidable bureaucracy containing, four deputy vice-chancellors; the proportion of university expenditure on administration was approximately twice what it would have been in a comparable UK university. The problem with this weight of bureaucracy, reinforced by the break-up of the unitary structure, was that the executive deans, who in practice had few executive powers, needed to obtain approvals for many administrative actions from the centre but had extraordinary difficulty in penetrating it to obtain decisions on quite trivial matters. The responsibilities of the deputy vice-chancellors overlapped and were not distinguished from those of the vice-chancellor while the large bureaucracy, which they allegedly controlled, exchanged memoranda and split hairs as to how to deal with simple issues. One result was that the deans began to develop their own administrations (in addition to the existing departmental administrations) in order to deal effectively with the bureaucracy at the centre, thus increasing the proportion of expenditure on administration and further draining the university's resources which could have been used to provide an orderly switch of resources from contracting to expanding faculties.

One conclusion to be drawn from this confusion was that the perception of the reforms that were needed was created at the centre and was based on a belief that the problems lay in the faculties and that reforms there could be achieved by parachuting in executive deans without going through the more difficult and contested process of changing the constitutional distribution of powers in respect to heads of departments and budgets, which would have required approval by the senate. No attempt had been made to reshape the central decision-making bodies, cut down the overblown central administration and transfer real powers to the faculties. On the contrary, the centre was seeking to shuffle off the tough decisions about restructuring departments from the centre, where they properly belonged, to the faculties without taking the trouble to face up to the prolonged arguments that would certainly have ensued if the deans were to have been given the constitutional powers that they required to do the job. Not surprisingly, the reforms stalled, and by a coincidence the vice-chancellor moved on to another post.

University C

University C is a UK civic university which had had a highly centralized management style dominated by an enveloping traditional committee structure and a large and bureaucratic central administration. It became clear in the 1990s that the university was not keeping pace with other universities of similar age and size and was in danger of slipping further in the RAE without internal academic rationalization and it took the opportunity of the appointment of a new and vigorous vice-chancellor to decide that it must embark on a radical overhaul in order to recapture its position. Most of these steps – the energetic engagement with local and regional economic ambitions to create new initiatives, the physical redevelopment of the campus, the investment in key academic activities – were successful but do not concern us here. But reforms in internal governance structures were seen as a key to unlocking the strengths of the university; these reforms covered similar ground to what was attempted in Universities A and B and it is instructive to compare successes and potential failures. The decision was taken to move from elected to executive deans, to be appointed by internal advertisement, not from outside as in University A; but coupled with this was the decision to change the faculty structure to reduce the number of faculties from seven to three, and to reduce some 50 or so departments to 30 schools. This meant that instead of imposing a new executive dean solution on an existing faculty structure, the whole internal organization was being changed, and internal legislative change, in terms of ordinances and regulations, proceeded side by side with organizational change, not as at university B. Moreover, unlike Universities A and B, the administrative 'Monday morning meeting' was replaced by an executive board, on which the new executive deans sat as *ex-officio* members, which acted under delegated powers in certain areas from the senate (itself a small representative body rather than an 'unreformed' senate on which all professors could sit as of right). The deans were therefore incorporated closely into the central decision-making process from the beginning. Finally, unlike University B, the central administration was heavily slimmed down in size, and a unitary registrar was appointed to pull the various departments into becoming a more focused organization; again, unlike University B, significant central functions were transferred to the new faculties which were encouraged to establish within devolved funding their own administrative structures.

The academic governance structure which then emerged was a form of collegiate university, each faculty representing a kind of college, which came together at the executive board and senate level to drive strategic change. The faculty board decision-making process remained knitted together with the centre by the board secretaries remaining on the registrar's staff, although paid for from the faculty budget. Longer term issues, however, revolve round the problems of maintaining a balance between corporate and faculty-based effectiveness. One sign of the success of the devolved structure can be seen in the decision to upgrade the title of dean to pro-vice-chancellor, thus putting the deans in status terms on the same level as the three central pro-vice-chancellors, but it could also be read as an indication of a shift in the balance of power relationships between the centre and the faculties. A sign of corporate imbalance might be seen in the pressure to increase administrative costs in the faculties as overlaps begin to occur with services provided by the centre and, at the next level down, of former departments retaining shadowy disciplinary entities within the new school structures. Ultimately, in terms of accountability and corporate decision-making, the central decision-making bodies need to retain a freedom of action, but this is going to be difficult unless the faculty 'barons' can continue, through the executive board and other bodies, to put institutional priorities above their own faculty concerns. The restructuring has contributed to a reinvigoration process but has yet to demonstrate that it is capable of moving the university decisively up the league tables.

University D

University D, another old UK civic university, presented an almost opposite story. Here an incoming vice-chancellor, presented with a traditional reporting mechanism where heads of departments reported notionally to the vice-chancellor, decided that the 54 departments should be merged, as at University C, into schools thus reducing the numbers reporting to the centre. In carrying through the reform, however, the school structure was imposed over, and did not replace, the departmental structure. However, this structure itself seemed in time to overload the reporting arrangements so the schools were merged into four faculties each headed by a provost, but once again this was a structure imposed over the schools which remained in being. While the provosts were closely involved in central decision-making, though not in such clearly defined mechanism as the executive board at University C, they found themselves heading a complex and highly layered decision-making process in their own faculties where departmental and school interests could block strategic decision-making, and foreclose on any attempt to achieve departmental rationalization in the face of low RAE scores. For the vice-chancellor, who had sought a more streamlined decision-making process, but who had not faced up to the confrontation that might have been involved at the senate level by abolishing old structures in parallel with creating new ones, the situation was, if anything, worse than before the first restructuring because a series of decision-making layers had been created which created absolute road blocks to change. Departments that attracted no students could rely on being defended by their colleagues at the different levels because any admission that failure to recruit students could be construed as a criteria for rationalization would open the floodgates to major academic restructuring. The university was in effect paralysed. Fortunately, the vice-chancellor reached retirement age and was replaced by someone who both de-layered the system and reached over what was left to use research performance as the main criterion for rationalization and voluntary redundancy. This had the effect, over time, of regenerating the university.

University E

When the polytechnics were freed from local authority control they found themselves with a minimum of financial reserves, at a considerable disadvantage as against the existing universities in their physical plant and with a market-orientated funding system set up by the Polytechnics and Colleges Funding Council (PCFC) which encouraged a rapid expansion of student numbers. Their new governing bodies were made up of hand-picked lay members mostly chosen from the business community who rightly recognized that economic viability represented a priority for management teams, who were necessarily inexperienced in the business of managing expanding institutions outside local authority control. This led to the widespread adoption of the executive dean principle with deans being recruited as line managers of groups of departments, given budgets and recruitment targets, and being made directly answerable for balancing their books to the chief executive. Failure to keep the faculty out of deficit and to pay an overhead charge to the institution could involve termination of appointment. Most deans were given permanent appointments subject to performance.

University E falls firmly into this category, although it might be said that its vice-chancellor, in adopting a heavily devolved structure, did so from a principled view of its value as an organizational model and deliberately kept the institution's central 'directorate' small. Indeed the university's multi-campus location in a mixed urban area bisected with freeways lent itself to this approach. But University E went further than most post-1992 institutions in also devolving student administration and quality management to the faculties as well as full responsibility for budgetary management. Each faculty had its own faculty finance officer and faculty registrar answerable exclusively to the dean. This was a much more clear-cut position than was adopted in University C, for example. In effect, what had been set up was a 'business' model with a board, a chief executive, who behaved like a chief executive, answerable to it, and devolved faculties, operating as subsidiary companies where the dean was a line manager answerable to the chief executive. Since the university was not research active the budgets were dominated by student-related funding and the performance measures were essentially to do with meeting student targets.

This structure suited the climate of 1992 well, but the environment changed. The unit of resource in national funding continued to decline making even limited success in the RAE an important source of recurrent finance; the translation of the teaching quality assessment (TQA) scores into league tables (along with RAE scores and student-related data) meant that low scoring condemned a non-research-active institution to a position in the lower quartile, with damaging consequences for reputation both locally and internationally; the new enthusiasm for initiative funding at the funding councils, particularly in 'third-stream' activities thrust a greater role on the centre; and the growing role of the regional development agencies in offering support to economically regenerative projects did not necessarily cohere with tightly drawn faculty structures. Increasingly the model became unfit for purpose: faculties were not investing differentially in areas which had research potential so the university continued to be unsuccessful in the RAE; some TQA scores were poor because the faculties had insufficient expertise to prepare for them so that quality management had to be pulled back to the centre; overseas student recruitment, and the income that went with it, suffered; student retention rates varied alarmingly between different faculty areas, with financial as well as academic consequences; third-stream and regional activities required central direction and cross-faculty engagement in a way not previously envisaged.

From the late 1990s the increasingly differentiated student market began to undermine the business model even further because some faculties lost numbers to the extent that they became non-viable while others expanded out of the space they had available on a dispersed campus. In addition the government's decision to encourage a more 'consumerist' student culture through its new fee and bursary policy imposed the need for stronger institutional policies in respect to 'customer care'; devolved services risked a failure to meet common standards.

In 2004 the vice-chancellor had to concede that his earlier vision needed amendment and that a greater degree of centralization had to be imposed. As he put it in a staff circular:

In an increasingly competitive environment I see no option but to achieve a greater degree of conformity and consistency and this can only be achieved by central direction and at the expense of individual faculty policies.

(University E, communication by the vice-chancellor
November 2004)

First, the faculty structure itself needed to be redrawn to merge or eliminate academic areas hit by declining intakes, but, second, faculty offices needed to be professionally linked to the central academic registry to ensure a conformity of services being offered in the faculties. Faculty finance officers would similarly be given a professional link to the central finance office to ensure better consistency in the management of university finance. All this would be accompanied by a rationalization of space, a merger of building and estates services and changing roles in the directorate.

The effect of these changes was not to unwind the devolved faculty structure but to rebalance it with the centre: the increasing marketization of higher education had increased the need for central control and the 'business model' of the 1990s of the holding company and its subsidies had to give way to something more akin to a unitary corporation with divisions. However, if research were to become a realistic component of some academic activities, it was almost certain that this would require yet more central involvement, both to ensure it was protected from the effect of falling student-related budgets, and to take advantage of regional or national initiatives. It might be concluded that the more a regional agenda too became dominant the stronger would be the need for central initiative which cross-cut and supplanted faculty priorities. Deans in this new model would become much more the executive arms of the centre than the champions of faculty initiative and the virtues of budgetary autonomy would be seen much less as a stimulus to self-reliance.

7

THE LESSONS TO BE LEARNT

A number of cross-cutting themes can be identified in the governance problems and issues listed in the previous chapter, but it is important to recognize the role that context played in each of the case studies. The Cardiff case could be seen as an example of institutional vulnerability to particular local pressures and circumstances under the old UGC 'hands off' approach. This it might be thought could not happen again under the more controlled governance arrangements of the post-1992 era were it not for the continuance of a funding council 'worry list' of institutions at risk. The problems at Cardiff, if they were to recur in 2006, would provide earlier warning signals, but external intervention would still be subject to legal constraint. The cumulative build up of bad management decision-making and ineffective governance is much more difficult to rectify than a single major failure. The decision by the Government to fast-track polytechnics and colleges out of local authority control in 1988 and into university or potential university status in 1992 without the financial support to underpin the market conditions that the Government had itself created as an instrument of policy put institutions under very great strain and it is not at all surprising that some failures occurred. The failure rate in higher education was much lower than in further education and it is notable that the institutions listed which faced difficulty all emerged stronger for the experience; Huddersfield and Portsmouth are effective institutions, the Southampton Institute has deservedly achieved full university status. Context was also important in the Lancaster case where the ambition to translate excellent RAE results into improved physical facilities outran the financial capacity of the institution and the competences of the staff involved. Context also played a considerable role in inspiring the academic governance changes in Universities A to E, where institutions were seeking to put themselves into better positions to counter market pressures. Perhaps what all this tells us is that university decision-making bodies need to be more proactive in considering the pressures of the external environment and how to adapt to them and governing bodies need a strategic framework within which to consider changes in governance structures and to monitor how such changes are actually working. Time spent on the reconnaissance of change is time well spent especially when compared to the turmoil and setbacks caused by blundering, unthinkingly, into radical departures which backfire. It is easy, after the event, of course, to say that if Lancaster had not been persuaded to reform its committee structure to streamline decision-making about university development, without first thinking about what development steps were necessary or if Cambridge had not in its Management Response to its external auditors seemingly washed its hands of trying to address its fundamental governance issue of reconciling autonomy at the departmental level with central authority before trying to create the financial system which was a necessary element of central authority, the crisis that hit both universities would not have occurred. Too often strategy in universities is reactive, based on the efforts of a senior group, perhaps in response to a partial interpretation of events, rather than determined by a joint committee of a governing body and a senate/academic board, which has invested time and energy in understanding the issues that their university faces and how to address them.

The dominant chief executive

In many of the cases described it is apparent that there was an imbalance between governance controls and the dominance of the vice-chancellor. In Cardiff, Huddersfield and the Southampton Institute it is clear that this dominance was actively supported either by the governing body itself or by a crucial subset of governors, so that, in effect, there was no critical or independent appraisal of decisions being taken. In all three cases strong-minded leaders shared their managerial objectives about institutional development with governors. At Cardiff there was unity around the objection to intervention from the UGC either in relation to institutional finance or to bring about a merger with UWIST; at Huddersfield there was no formal dissent from the creation of a corporate model of governance which excluded staff and students and the decision to award the vice-chancellor such generous retirement terms is a testimony to the extent the governors shared his vision of how the university had progressed; at the Southampton Institute the director worked so closely with his chair, vice-chair and chair of resources committee that the rest of the governing body felt excluded from any serious participation in decision-making. At Lancaster, where the position was by no means so clear cut, it was, nevertheless, the dominance of the vice-chancellor over the reformed committee structure and over his officers which created the conditions for a financial crisis. Rowe makes the point very clearly that the university council and its officers 'may not have acted with sufficient frequency and firmness to test the proposals laid before it' (Rowe 1997 *ibid* j).

What we see in these instances is the danger to institutional integrity implicit in the passive governing body described by Bennett (2002) when there is no counter-balance to the power of a dominant chief executive. If one of the chief responsibilities of a governing body is the appointment of a vice-chancellor, exercising control over policy when a vigorous chief executive wishes to press ahead with new activities represents a different and equally demanding responsibility, especially for a group of essentially non-executive directors who may not be close to the evidence of cumulative risk involved in some of them. Appraisal processes involving the chair of the governing body are, of course, part of this control mechanism but such exercises, conducted annually, are not likely to be anything like so effective as a robust governing body which asks critical questions and shows independence of mind in seeking information to support institutional policies. Universities need vigorous vice-chancellors who can confront issues and chart policies for change and adaptation to environmental pressures, but they also need members of governing bodies who bring an independence of thought to decision-making and who are willing to challenge the dominant consensus. Evidence from the US confirms that these issues are equally relevant in universities with a long tradition of powerful lay boards (Chait *et al* 1991, 1996).

In the civic university constitution, tradition would suggest that the chief challenge to the over-dominant chief executive might come at the senate level, but in modern conditions this is less likely: senates are usually too large and the cumulative detail of university business does not throw up issues at that level which are large enough to provoke a major confrontation with a vice-chancellor, although the senate's decision at Warwick in 2005 to refuse to support the establishment of a separate campus in Singapore suggests that when the decision is big enough senates can reassert themselves. Where, at Cardiff, a senate did seek to exercise control over its vice-chancellor, it was not supported by its council. In such circumstances the real controls over impetuous actions by a chief executive can only be exercised by those who have command of the complex information involved: these will be the university's professional officers or a senior management team written into the university's governance machinery as at Strathclyde and Warwick (see page 67) or at University C. The case study universities referred to above not only had passive governing bodies but lacked the machinery or organizational culture to exercise such controls. At Cardiff the pliability of the senior professional officers, and the principal's ability to create new senior administrative posts outside internal regulations or a budget framework ensured that he was able to operate in a wholly unconstrained manner. Neither the Huddersfield nor the Southampton Institute HEC constitutions offered any support to officers who offered contrary views to their chief executives, a position reinforced by the departure, in different circumstances, of the deputy vice-chancellor of Portsmouth. At Lancaster the director of finance was publicly rebuked for challenging the views of his vice-chancellor. None of these institutions had a UMG, a steering committee or an executive board where senior academics and administrators conversant with the detail could challenge a vice-chancellor in open debate on a particular issue in the knowledge that such a disagreement would, in a minuted discussion, be reported to senates or governing bodies.

Where difficulties have occurred involving over-dominant chief executives it has been the academic community rather than governing bodies that have been the primary agents for change. At Huddersfield, Portsmouth and the Southampton Institute, and at Cardiff, academic bodies have passed votes of no confidence or held meetings reported in the media, but these have always occurred after the event not at the point when bad decisions were being made. While these incidents emphasize the importance of academic involvement in university governance, they are not effective in the way that a strong form of 'cabinet government' can be in ensuring that the complex decisions that may have to be taken at the governing body level have been properly explored and subjected to sustained and expert discussion. The Lancaster council may have had three sets of lawyers present to advise its members on the bond issue, but the definitive analysis of the affair which highlighted the interrelationship of poor governance practice, bad decision-making and lack of professional competence which created the crisis in the University's affairs was conducted by a group of academics, under the chairmanship of a professor of law. It was the absence of that level of discussion, as events occurred, which permitted an avoidable breakdown to take place.

Ambiguity in governance and management structures ■

A lack of clarity in governance and management structures can also be seen to have been contributed substantially to governance problems. The case that stands out here is Cambridge, where not only were three committees involved in the Capsa failure but none of them carried formal responsibility. The finance committee and the planning and resources committee were separately involved in commissioning the exercise, the planning and resources committee for allocating resources and approving a project manager, the finance committee for approving the preferred supplier and setting the implementation date. In addition there was a steering committee for the project which was not, however, charged to manage it. The confusion was paralleled by ambiguity over officer control with the registrary's position as unitary head of the administration compromised by the University's unwillingness to place the treasurer, who had started the project, formally under the registrary's control so that while the director of management information services reported to the registrary the new director of finance who undertook the implementation never knew whether her line responsibility was to the treasurer or the registrary.

One might argue that Cambridge represents something of a special case, but similar confusion beset the Lancaster situation with the professional administrative officers failing to act in a coordinated way so that activities were pressed forward in respect to new buildings, the takeover of the Charlotte Mason College and a premature retirement scheme which were never subjected to an overall financial assessment of the cash flow implications, The activities were being driven executively by committees chaired by pro-vice-chancellors but the financial implications were not controlled by the finance and general purposes committee which, itself, had to leave critical approvals to its chair because of the timetable problems. The council itself was brought in to provide signatures for the bond without being adequately involved in the considerations which necessitated it. Responsibility for initiating action was diffused between committees and officers and between professional officers and pro-vice-chancellors, so that while the council might have been *de jure* responsible, neither it nor the committee to which it had delegated its responsibilities had *de facto* control.

Similar confusions afflicted the Southampton Institute where a resource committee was given delegated powers but met so infrequently that critical business ventures were launched by a combination of university officers in consultation with the chair and vice-chair of the committee. The responses by governing body members to the questionnaire circulated by HEFCE's auditors provides clear evidence of the extent to which members felt themselves distanced from critical decision-making. At Portsmouth the removal of the deputy vice-chancellor and his planned substitution by a professional finance person, the entanglement of this issue with the accusations about the inappropriate behaviour of the vice-chancellor, the action by the audit committee in behaving as a disciplinary body, and the failure to inform the governing body, all represent, albeit in difficult circumstances, a confusion of roles and procedures which compounded the problems the University was facing. And at Univerities A and B the ambiguities in the relations between the deans, their faculties and the universities' central decision-making processes lay at the heart of the difficulties that emerged.

There is no doubt that well-understood governance structures, defined terms of reference for committees and agreed delegations of powers bring clarity to decision-making because they impose a process and a timetable to the conduct of university business and an assurance that there has been appropriate levels of consideration of important issues. At the same time the interrelationship between governance and management requires that managers and administrators have clear lines of communication and reporting, both horizontally as well as vertically. It is also imperative that the governance culture imposes on professional officers a responsibility to express themselves positively or negatively on issues at decision-making bodies if they feel obliged on professional grounds to do so. It is especially the case that in complex financial decision-making the impartial advice of a professionally qualified university officer can be of critical importance because the decision-makers will probably not themselves be experts in the area and may not have fully comprehended the ramifications of the facts placed before them.

The role of university administrators ▮

In the 1960s, when the move towards greater academic participation in university governance was at its height, the vice-chancellor of Essex, in his Reith Lectures, coined the phrase 'an academic civil service' to describe the role of a university administrator (Sloman 1964). The Franks Report, reflecting Oxford's concerns that administrators were becoming too powerful in the University's complex structure, offered soothing comfort in the following:

> The value of an efficient civil service in a university is that it makes it possible, even with a complicated structure, to practise

democratic control by academics of the policies that shape their environment.

(University of Oxford 1964 *ibid* b)

Times have changed and more is required of university administrators in managing the large and costly organizations that universities have become. Helen Thorley, an administrator at Lancaster, sums up the administrators' role in the Lancaster crisis as:

> Our vast, totally representative and meticulously serviced committee structure of the early 1990s apparently failed to spot the dangers ahead or even to ask the appropriate questions about viability. With very few exceptions, committees assumed that all the plans were all right, presumably because those paid to advise them – the administrators didn't explicitly tell them otherwise.
>
> (Thorley 1998 a)

On the basis of the Lancaster experience she concludes:

> As a committee secretary or an 'officer in attendance' you are not just there to take the minutes or to speak only when spoken to. You must ensure the right information is presented, you must correct matters of fact, you must be pro-active in the debate – and you must be prepared to say so when you believe someone is leading the committee to a decision which is not in the interests of the institution.
>
> (Thorley *ibid* b)

As we have seen above the finance director attempted to do this but the general thrust of what Thorley is saying is important. In Cardiff, in general in Lancaster, in Huddersfield and in Portsmouth, university administrators who could see things going wrong did not speak out, while in Cambridge they in effect looked away as the crisis built up. Of all the institutions quoted, only in the Southampton Institute did an administrator make clear his concern when the director of corporate affairs seems to have led a deputation to the chair and, perhaps underlining the risks involved, then took voluntary redundancy (Brown 2003c). Nevertheless, uncomfortable though the precedent may be, university administrators do have a necessary role in registering their disquiet and advising publicly against actions they believe to be unwise. The protection to the position of the secretary to the governing body, as described in the CUC *Guide* (see page 23–25) reflects a recognition of the extent to which the post of secretary can be politically exposed.

Audit processes ▪

The Cardiff case in 1987 precipitated a concern for audit in the higher education sector generally and the subsequent concerns in commerce and industry from the Robert Maxwell affair through to Enron have emphasized the importance of appropriate audit arrangements as part of the corporate governance machinery. At Cardiff there was no internal audit machinery, no audit committee and the external auditors were loyal to the university to the extent of declining to cooperate with the Price Waterhouse inquiry imposed by the accounting officer for the university system. What the Cardiff affair exposed was the extent to which the state's resources could be placed at risk by maverick institutional behaviour and the need for proper audit processes to be made a requirement of public funding. The problem with effective audit arrangements in well managed, financially sound institutions is that they can easily be represented to be costly and bureaucratic: audit committees can be portrayed as time wasting and nit picking and the response to external auditors' management letters as rebuffs to unjustified interventions into autonomous institutional practices.

But the value of audit, whether the comments of an audit committee or the reports of internal or external auditors, is that they emanate from sources which are functionally detached from the institution and therefore constitute an impartial view. This is not to say that the view is always the correct one or that the process may not miss identifying some core weakness, but in the often internalized and tunnel-visioned world of university decision-making, such as is exemplified in the Lancaster, Cambridge and Southampton Institute cases, the impartial external assessment of the facts can be an important corrective and can give confidence and support to those who have doubts over a particular course of action. Unfortunately, audit recommendations tend to be made some months after the crucial events and it is rare that institutions choose to involve the audit process as a situation is developing.

The Cambridge case in many ways represents a classic articulation of audit failure. This failure was not, however, the result of the absence of audit warnings both from the internal and the external auditors, but arose from the unwillingness of the University and its senior officers to take these warnings seriously and from the fact that the audit committee as a consequence of its membership, which comprised members and former members of staff of the University, was so internal to the University's activities that it did not recognize the force of the warnings when delivered and would probably have lacked the standing with the council to have achieved the necessary reforms even if it had had the courage to demand them. But audit weakness is apparent in a high proportion of the case studies. At Lancaster there appears to have been no audit scrutiny of the processes involved in procuring the bond or in the absence of machinery to monitor cash flow. The acquiring of Charlotte Mason College and the lack of a due diligence report was not subject to adverse comment, even after the event. At the Southampton Institute the unsuccessful overseas venturing, accompanied as it was in respect to the Athens campus by a great deal of adverse publicity, was never the subject of adverse reports to the governing body. At Huddersfield it was left to the NAO, reacting to ferocious external publicity, to comment adversely on the *ultra vires* financial package offered to the outgoing vice-chancellor, while at Portsmouth the audit committee abrogated to itself powers which it did not possess and failed to report adequately its findings.

In all these cases if the audit machinery had worked properly considerable institutional damage could have been avoided. But in these cases, and in most universities, the value of the external voice which audit provides is underestimated. Membership of audit committees is not prized, the chairmanship of such a committee is onerous, and in the current climate becoming much more so, and can carry with it a degree of unpopularity because much of the committee's work is asking questions which are thought to be unnecessary by those responding to them, or raising issues in a way that may impose unacceptable delays on operations already in progress. For audit committees to be truly effective their membership needs to be carefully selected from governors, perhaps reinforced by some complete outsiders, who have had operational experience in management and are sympathetic to the objectives of universities and their role needs to be understood and supported by the university's management. For a chairman of a governing body or of a finance committee or for a vice-chancellor, however, an effective audit machinery offers the best reassurance that the affairs of the institution are soundly based and that the risks endemic in any successful operation have been understood and taken into account.

Responsibility for the effective management of institutional resources

The Financial Memorandum lays on governing bodies responsibility for ensuring that they have a sound system of financial control. This can be interpreted in a narrow technical sense but the terms of the charters, statutes and articles of government flesh this out in wider terms and impose managerial responsibilities which go beyond fiduciary responsibility in the narrow sense to a duty to ensure the overall effective management of resources. Governing bodies rarely take time to consider this duty, their agendas being overwhelmed by the need to approve individual recommendations about the detailed management and development of their institutions. They may well seek assurances about the effectiveness of the financial systems, but these systems are only one aspect of a wider question of managerial effectiveness. Many of the case studies illustrate very clearly the failure of governing bodies to consider the organizational factors which underpin financial control mechanisms. Cardiff, of course, represents a prime example of a governing body which simply, and without critical consideration, accepted the promptings of its principal, ignoring the evidence of financial collapse that was stacking up before it. Cambridge, where under its statutes the council is responsible for the 'administration' of the University, took pride in the economy with which the University was centrally managed and gave no thought to the broader issue that an administration starved of resources and lacking a unified command structure would place the University at risk when it tried to install a comprehensive financial control system of a level of sophistication not previously envisaged. In Lancaster similarly the question never seemed to have been asked as to whether, bearing in mind the loss of senior staff, the University had the capacity to take on so many and various projects and bring them to fruition successfully while at the same time pioneering a novel financial mechanism to fund them on which there was no previous experience in the sector. At Portsmouth the decision to reorganize the directorate and bring in a professional finance director replacing a deputy vice-chancellor was taken by the vice-chancellor and the chair of governors without discussion by the governing body of the reorganization implications for the formulation of policy which this implied.

The management of academic resources

The argument in the section above can be extended to questions of academic organization in so far as this might raise resource management issues. Indeed the civic university statutes, while placing responsibility on senates for academic performance, are very clear that questions of academic organization – a faculty reorganization or a closure of a department – are matters that must be approved by the council, albeit after consultation with the senate. In HEC's the unitary powers of governing bodies over educational as well as managerial and financial matters gives governing bodies an even more important responsibility for determining academic organizational issues. Despite this, governing bodies are almost invariably passive in regard to such issues. At the Southampton Institute two academic reorganizations had been allowed to occur in two years and the director announced a third reorganization without consulting the governors at all. In University B the council allowed confusion to occur in administrative decision-making and approved a botched academic reorganization that failed. In University D an academic organization was permitted to grow up which it was abundantly clear was over-complicated, wasteful of resources and not fit for purpose. Governing bodies need to be pro-active in reviewing the organizational context in which detailed financial control mechanisms operate or, as in many of the cases described above, they will find that in particular moments of stress it will no longer deliver the security which is required.

But such responsibilities need to be shared with the academic community which should play a full part in considering what are the structures that can best deliver academic processes. Unless their senates and academic boards are fully engaged in critical discussion of changes in academic organization, important issues are likely to be overlooked for this reason. Governing bodies of HECs should always seek advice from their academic boards before agreeing to restructuring proposals, even though legally there is no requirement for them to do so. The examples of Universities B and D, where senates approved academic governance changes in which serious governance malfunctions were to emerge, show that consultation does not always eliminate shortcomings but it does have the benefit of gaining a readier acceptance of the need for change.

The centre and the basic academic units

Problems of communication and decision-making linkages between the centre and the units responsible for teaching and research lie at the heart of the dilemmas of academic organization. In some universities the centre–department axis remains paramount; in others size and complexity have replaced this with centre–faculty/school relationships creating a further faculty/school–disciplinary relationship at another level down. The role of a dean as the intermediary between the centre and the academic unit is critical to the process working well. Universities A and B illustrate problems of legitimacy in the position of the dean where the deans remained isolated between the centre and the faculties with ambiguous relations with both. Universities C and E, however, raise questions as to the distribution of managerial powers between the centre and the faculties with in University D evidence of managerial powers leaking out of the centre to the faculties and in University E the university trying to recentralize power and direction in the light of its perception of a changing environment. In all these universities factors of mission, size and disciplinary base, together with organizational history, play a part in determining the most appropriate structure. However, creating the right machinery, determining the appropriate balance of power distribution, and deciding whether the dean is a member of the senior management team, as in University C, or a suppliant to it, as in universities A and B, represent essential issues of university governance. The failure to align central policy perceptions with the academic dynamics of an institution and *vice versa* can lie at the heart of problems in academic governance.

The management of due process

A thread which runs through so many of the case studies is failings in the management of due process, in the efficient 'servicing' of committees, or in the lack of implementation of decisions taken: at Cardiff and at Cambridge committee decisions were taken to set up sinking funds, in Cardiff for the new telephone system, in Cambridge for the new financial system, but neither decision was implemented and the committees concerned did not receive reports that this was the case. At Cambridge a very critical report from the internal auditors setting out their doubts about the Capsa implementation date was never forwarded to the Capsa steering committee which was therefore kept in ignorance of the views of the University's professional advisers. At Lancaster the working parties set up to oversee each project did not keep minutes and failed to report to the estates committee so that an ambitious building programme was allowed to get out of control. The Lancaster council was inadequately briefed by its secretariat and professional officers so that the moment when a cash flow crisis could have been avoided by the delay of a particular project was missed. These failures were symptomatic of more general professional shortcomings in the way business was conducted, how committees communicated, how decisions were recorded and actioned and what advice to committees was given.

It would be easy to conclude that these failings point to a need for universities to turn to more executive styles of management where individuals are accountable for their actions rather than committees, except that in the HEC case studies, where the constitutions favoured an executive style, the weaknesses endemic when appropriate controls on impetuous conduct are not in place, show that other risks may be involved. Both styles of governance need professional support to be effective. In all the cases where real governance breakdowns occurred deficiencies in the professional support and in the ability of the secretary of the university to play an independent role are apparent. In Cardiff, Lancaster and Cambridge, as we have seen, there were technical shortcomings in the way business was conducted. At Cardiff the situation was compounded by the fact that the registrar was also a deputy Principal and therefore closely associated with the dominant management style. At Lancaster, the departure of an experienced secretary and professional team and the vice-chancellor's personal role in reshaping the management team made the exercise of an independent voice and administrative coordination difficult to achieve. The action to silence the finance director's comments should, however, have alerted the secretary to his responsibility to provide independent advice to the chair of the governing body. At Cambridge the failure to unify the administration under the registrary and the resistance by some members of the academic community to any form of administrative coordination severely weakened the registrary's ability to ensure that business was conducted effectively. Indeed the Capsa affair, besides illustrating ineffective governance, provides a case study of what can happen in the management of a demanding project when it is attempted under a divided command.

But in the Cardiff, and in the Huddersfield, Portsmouth and Southampton Institute cases real questions also arise about the independent role of the secretary to the governing body because in each case serious procedural errors of governance took place. At Cardiff the registrar had a duty to make clear to the council the legal and financial implications of the permanent secretary's intervention and requirement that the University cooperate fully with the Price Waterhouse inquiry. Events at Huddersfield, Portsmouth and the Southampton Institute demonstrate very clearly the lack of strong independent guidance on procedural and legal issues: the vice-chancellor's retirement package at Huddersfield, the handling of the potential conflicts of interest in relation to the deputy vice-chancellor's departure and the allegations of inappropriate behaviour by the vice-chancellor at Portsmouth, or the conduct of governing body business at the Southampton Institute all demonstrate a lack of respect for due process, and for the proper conduct of public business.

Good governance in universities needs well-informed and independent-minded participants, whether on governing bodies, senates or academic boards or lower bodies supported by secretariats and professional officers who coordinate business and ensure it is conducted according to approved procedures. It is a characteristic of university committee structures, whether a governing body or a faculty board, that the great majority of the members will be non-executive rather than executive members and in these circumstances the role of the university secretary is to ensure that members are properly informed, that decision-making bodies do not exceed their powers, that decisions are appropriately recorded and implemented and that higher bodies duly receive the recommendations made to them. In the cases above where serious governance breakdowns occurred the support services also failed.

8

MANAGING GOOD
GOVERNANCE IN PRACTICE

Appointing a vice-chancellor

Most universities will agree that the most important action a university governing body can take is the appointment of a vice-chancellor, which makes it surprising that there is so little written about the process in the UK. (The Universities UK guide to best practice in appointing senior managers is too bland and politically correct to be useful except as a guide for the avoidance of legal action by candidates (Universities UK 2004).) In the civic university model the responsibility is shared between the governing body and the senate and the appointing machinery is characteristically a joint committee with the appointment being subject to consultation with the senate before a final decision is taken by the governing body. In at least one instance in recent times a senate has voted down the nomination from a joint committee, a decision which the governing body respected, and recommenced the appointing process. Such a situation could not arise at an HEC where the appointment is the governors' alone, although some academic representation is normally included in the appointing committee. In either case, considerable responsibility rests on the chair and, to a lesser extent, on the secretary of the committee because, particularly in the past, before the employment of professional executive search organizations, they handled all the detailed correspondence and arrangements with candidates. However, even now the burden of responsibility and the requirements for face-to-face meetings are heavy and no chair (or secretary) who has not the time to devote to the exercise should take it on. Members of the appointing committee, normally selected to provide some balance of interests, should also make the exercise a diary priority because with at any time at least ten universities looking or being about to look for a vice-chancellor, the flexibility of arranging meetings, without critical absences, when there is a competition for the best candidates, is essential.

With the increasing use of executive search organizations, universities may have speeded up the process and improved the professionalism in seeking out appropriate candidates, but they are also in danger of handing over the process to an external organization. It should also be remembered that 'head hunters' like estate agents derive their income from the 'purchase decision' of the clients and whatever their protestations, their ultimate business success is for an appointment to be made, rather than the most suitable appointment being made for the institution. There should always be a selection process for 'head hunters' where the appointing committee can decide whether they respect the judgement and methods of the agents who are involved. (A worst case scenario can be when the chair imposes an executive search firm, which he/she has worked with in a company situation, but which may not have the background, sensitivity to the university's needs, or the appropriate experience and contacts to deliver a broad list of candidates). Universities should never rely on 'head hunters' alone for identifying potential candidates but should actively engage in a search exercise themselves. Committees need to decide what parts of the process they want the 'head hunter' for: creating a long list, contacting people knowledgeable about the candidates, drawing up a shortlist or even up to arranging the interviews. Some 'head hunters' can become so dominant in the process that the committee only sees curriculum vitae and personal assessments drawn up by the 'head hunter' and take no real part in the process before they face a candidate across an interview table. Best practice suggests that 'head hunters' should be used only for what they are good at – assembling a first list of candidates and persuading candidates to allow their names to be considered – so that the university retains a secure grip on its own decision-making process. Appointing committees should never allow themselves, whatever a candidate might intimate, to be sidetracked from making their own enquiries, particularly by academic members speaking in confidence to colleagues in a candidate's own institution, so that the committee has full ownership of the personal judgements that have to be made. Interview styles may also vary between, at one extreme, the straight job interview kind of approach, where several candidates are seen on the same day enabling comparisons to be easily made, to, at the other, the more conversational approach, one at a time, where a more detailed exchange of views can take place. Variations can be where each committee member has a separate conversation with candidates before a final meeting with the full committee or where a group of senior academics who are not members of the appointing committee, perhaps the pro-vice-chancellors or deans, have a prior opportunity of meeting the candidates, and reporting their views to the committee.

Two important subsidiary points need to be made. The first is that the appointee needs to be able to work with the senior management team that exists (in the US a university president generally has the freedom to bring in his/her own team if that is thought desirable). The most outstanding candidate may not fit the institution or its decision-making process and may be likely to waste energy and resources on organizational disruption, which could be better spent on forwarding the institution's interests. The second is that in the UK, at least, the number of candidates appointed from within their own university is extremely small whereas in industry and commerce the figure for managing director posts is about 80 per cent. The university may seek an external candidate because it is looking for change, but however diligent the process of appointment there must always be an element of risk in bringing in someone with whom no one has had a prior working relationship. An internal candidate, on the other hand, can be judged on past performance and, although it can be argued that the danger of an internal appointment is that the appointee in office may be influenced by past alliances and friendship with colleagues, this does not seem to have discouraged the practice in other organizations. Many universities have cause to lament that former staff have left to lead other institutions more successfully than their present incumbent.

Finally, it is important that the chair, with the secretary, establishes clearly both with the appointing committee and with the remuneration committee in advance the terms of any offer to the successful candidate and any limitations on flexibility so that negotiation can be conducted effectively and proposals, for example, for deferring take up for a year, obtaining a post for a wife or partner, or maintaining two households while childrens' school examinations are completed can be responded to with confidence and a candidate can be left with no uncertainty where the institution stands. Candidates in this situation often reveal sides to their character which have not previously been apparent and the chair needs to be secure in his/her negotiating position so that there is no difficulty in moving on to consider another candidate.

Monitoring the executive ■

It is expected that a governing body will monitor the performance of the executive, and particularly of the vice-chancellor, but analogies with the private sector are dangerous. The remunerated chair of a company board will be familiar with the company's business and its business environment and his/her hand is strengthened by being answerable to shareholders. A chair of governors, on the other hand, receives no recompense (the single case referred to in the Lambert Review has not, in fact, been realized), is not usually an expert in the business and, under CUC guidelines, is not likely to serve for more than six years.

Moreover, measuring performance when that performance may be circumscribed, in the case of the pre-1992 universities by senates, and in all universities by the individual academic performance of staff, is less easy than using measures relating to production, profitability and shareholder return. It needs also to be remembered that the chair of governors/vice-chancellor relationship must include the existence of a running two-way dialogue. The chair is perhaps the only person who the vice-chancellor can talk to about difficulties and problems, and frankness will not be encouraged on such occasions if it is felt that these are being noted down to be reproduced later at an appraisal meeting. Chairs may seem omniscient but may need help from the vice-chancellor in piloting through the governing body unpopular proposals. Chairs and vice-chancellors have to work in harmony. This does not mean that monitoring performance should not be attempted, but does suggest that it should be approached with care. One golden rule is to start a process with a new vice-chancellor the way it is intended to continue. If, for example, the chair believes in 360-degree assessment, difficult as it may be in a university context, it should be done from the beginning and not introduced after some years when a vice-chancellor may see it as a reflection on performance. A more effective approach may be to require a vice-chancellor to offer a list of targets which can be reviewed at the end of each year. In some universities the remuneration committee itself sets targets for vice-chancellors.

Although formally such monitoring is the responsibility of the chair, there may be value in involving one or two other senior members of the governing body. This has the effect of de-personalizing the process and gives the chair a small forum where opinions can be shared and alternative views expressed. It may be especially desirable, if there is any danger of a dominant chief executive emerging, as described in some of the case studies. Where the monitoring process covers other senior executives, as it often will do in HECs, broadening the participation is essential. Monitoring performance leads naturally to questions of remuneration which must formally be handled by the remuneration committee. This committee should receive a report from the chair of governors on the monitoring process if it is to conduct its business fairly. The annual release of data on vice-chancellors' emoluments in the institutional accounts and their collating *Times Higher Education Supplement* (2006) has an inflationary effect and does not always suggest that this is a very testing process, especially as the gap between vice-chancellors' and academic salaries increases.

Effectiveness and performance reviews

Effectiveness reviews of governing bodies and performance reviews conducted by governing bodies were recommended by Dearing and endorsed by Lambert and have become part of the machinery which governing bodies have adopted to give assurance that they take their role seriously. The effectiveness review, based on questionnaire returns from members (but not from people outside the governing body) have been valuable in providing an outlet for the views of members on the governance process and, as the CUC *Review of University Governance 1997–2000* (CUC 2000b) makes clear, have served to highlight for governing bodies significant areas where in individual institutions improvements could be made. The review of the questionnaire responses by a specially appointed committee with some external membership was also recognized as good practice. The CUC has rightly recommended that such reviews should be conducted every five years rather than the three years recommended by Lambert. However, there should be caution in placing too great a reliance on internal effectiveness reviews as machinery which gives assurance that effectiveness is being maintained. In the US, where such mechanisms have been employed for longer Holland found in a study of the self assessments conducted by 61 non-profit boards that every one concluded that it was performing above the average (Holland 1991).

There is an element of management faddism (Birnbaum 2000) and box-ticking (Hampel 1998) in the importance that is ascribed to the effectiveness review process and it is perhaps for this reason that it has not been adopted by senates and academic boards. They are wrong, however, not to do so. If governing bodies have found them useful, as they have, senates and academic boards should take their own processes of decision-making seriously enough to follow suit. The perception quoted in Lambert of university decision-making being 'slow moving, bureaucratic and risk averse' (Lambert 2003 g) may be based on anecdotal or selective evidence but at least could be rebutted with more confidence if effectiveness reviews had been introduced in relation to academic decision-making. If senates and academic boards are to play an active role with governing bodies in university governance they need to submit themselves to comparable review processes.

Performance reviews raise different issues. At one level the expectation must be that if a governing body is to approve a strategic plan it is difficult to do so without reviewing performance over the past year against academic and financial targets. Performance review is thus an ongoing process, inextricably linked with strategy reviews. At least one university, Warwick, presents for discussion at both its senate and council a complex digest of institutional and national statistics constructed so that performance in student recruitment, retention and completion, by academic programme and subsequent employment, in winning research grants and contracts, in publication rates etc. by academic departments, with substantial time series, which is compared with national data, so that issues of variable performance can be addressed. Parallel data on financial performance are issued each year by the funding councils against an agreed set of performance indicators. The CUC publishes some case studies of performance review processes, but these are not convincing because they are dependent on internal target-setting which does not explicitly take account of where the institution stands in relation to national data (CUC 2004e).

If formal performance reviews are to become a necessary element of quality assurance for good governance it is essential that they are undertaken jointly with the academic community. So-called KPIs can be dangerously simplistic and are open to many different interpretations – do low 'A' level scores denote a reputational deficit or a determination to widen access? does high expenditure on a library represent a necessary commitment to research, an over-provision of staff as against materials, or even an over-expenditure on periodicals concealing an under-expenditure on student texts? does low expenditure on building maintenance demonstrate efficiency or underprovision? Senates/academic boards and governing bodies have a common interest in establishing and assessing performance levels, which should not simply be defined by senior management. Performance reviews need to be undertaken professionally and appropriate resources need to be allocated to ensure that the necessary data are captured and compared. The UK has, in the Higher Education Statistics Agency (HESA) data base, the most comprehensive set of higher education statistics of any European country and inter-

institutional and national subject area comparisons can be inter-
rogated to provide a clear picture of where a university stands in
comparison with other institutions of like characteristics. If a governing body is to embark on such an exercise in conjunction with its
senate/academic board it needs to determine in advance how it is
going to use the findings. Performance reviews should be integral to
strategy formation and should not be exercises undertaken for their
own sake or they will consume resources without producing any
return other than ticking a governance box. In other words if governing bodies embark on performance reviews they should see them
as embodying a commitment to action with the results feeding into
discussions about the institution's strategic planning and to the reviews of executive performance. Formal performance reviews should
be undertaken at regular intervals, using common data sets with time
series so that trends can be identified; many universities, on the
other hand, may feel that they should be undertaken annually as part
of the strategic planning process itself. In either case it is imperative
that the review report be available throughout the institution and
not restricted to the commissioning body. This is not just because
transparency can instil a sense of ownership of successes and problem areas across the institution but because an open discussion of
such issues can generate an organizational culture which will respond positively to strategy-driven change.

Away days

A common approach to dealing with strategic issues is to organize an
away day to discuss them. The positive arguments for such events are
that it gives busy members of a committee or a management team an
opportunity to discuss complex material in a more considered way
than would be the case in the normal round of meetings. The danger
is that the whole process of taking decision-makers away from their
normal venue and creating an artificial atmosphere of leisure to
consider big issues can have such a liberating effect that the conclusions reached are unrealistic and do not reflect the pressures of the
day-to-day which would have informed them if they had been trying
to reach decisions through the normal meetings schedule. Some of
the worst strategic decisions, the ones that people ask in retrospect
how they had ever been made, have been made at away days. Away
days can be a useful means of education for decision-makers and can
be helpful in integrating new members or encouraging contributions
to discussion from members who perhaps find the formal processes
of senior committees rather daunting, but time for reflection should

always be left between away day conclusions and final decisions and these final decisions should be taken in the ambiance of the normal decision-making process. In particular strategy planning, and strategic decisions, should always be taken against a background of financial planning where hard choices have to be made between alternative courses of action which have been subjected to rigorous financial review. Away day enthusiasms can too often minimize the discipline imposed by professional inputs to decision-making.

Financial control

Governing bodies are responsible for the financial health of an institution and in a formal sense they carry this out through approving a financial plan and an annual budget and ensuring, through their audit committees, that procedures for risk management, control and governance systems and monitoring are in place (CUC *ibid* f). Normally, a governing body will have a finance or finance and general purposes committee, which may have some delegated powers of decision-making, but which a governing body relies upon for expert financial advice. The members will be chosen accordingly. A finance, and particularly a finance and general purposes committee meeting four or five times a year can be expected to have a full agenda and to regard its monitoring function as restricted to receiving regular reports from the director of finance or even quarterly accounts. University financial management is, however, complicated by the variety of income sources and the large number of expenditure outlets, including many which have unpredictable patterns of expenditure (especially in research intensive universities) which can make accurate cash flow forecasting difficult. There are strong arguments for a finance committee to establish a special budget monitoring group, perhaps made up of some members and some officers, whose task should be to scrutinize income and expenditure, broken down into budget heads, on a two-monthly basis. One value of this is that the finance committee can reassure itself that it has a real grip on how the annual budget plan is proceeding and whether the target surplus will be met. But another is that such machinery gives the finance committee confidence to make flexible changes to the budget as the year progresses and, if required, to approve new initiatives requiring unbudgeted institutional investment. Perhaps most important it provides both a check on the director of finance as well as a forum at which he/she can express concerns about the pressures the budget is coming under due to circumstances which were not foreseen or foreseeable at the time it was drawn up. Such machinery greatly strengthens the hand of the chair of finance committee in reporting to the governing body. If it had been in place at Cardiff and Lancaster their financial respective difficulties need not have occurred because it would have provided the early warnings to their finance committees that their finances were sliding out of control.

Audit committee

The importance of audit in modern governance arrangements is described in Chapter 3. In a university setting there are particular difficulties in establishing an effective audit committee: the post of committee chair is not attractive to well-qualified lay members because it excludes them from playing a role on key committees like finance or building which seem more central to the university's future; to find other governing body members who are willing and able to ask tough questions of the executive may also be difficult. The high fees that have to be paid to non-executive members of company boards only emphasizes the unattractiveness of the role. A university is wise always to have at least two members of an audit committee who are not members of a governing body, simply as a way of ensuring that the committee is able to draw on a sufficiently wide range of expertise. This approach can also be used as a way of involving external members as a preliminary to inviting them on to full membership of the governing body in due course. The importance of appointing members of experience and standing to an audit committee can be judged by the difficulties at Portsmouth and the committee's unwillingness to rock the boat at Cambridge.

Universities have the choice of appointing their own in-house team or employing an outside firm to undertake the internal audit function. Large universities may well prefer the former approach because, if an able team can be recruited, it can develop an understanding of the institution which makes it much more effective than an external team: it is available at all times, it can cross-reference from one part of an institution to another, it can fulfill an important advisory role and it has consistency of personnel. On the other hand, reporting mechanisms and questions of independence and impartiality can often be raised in relation to internal teams. At Cambridge the appointed internal auditor identified all the right questions but her warnings were ignored; but her replacement by an employed external firm achieved no better a result. The internal team has the benefit of being readily available to comment on new systems or give advice on difficult issues. It is hard to imagine that an internal auditor would not have commented adversely on the decision at Lancaster to allow its adviser on options for financing its building programme to become its agent for raising the debenture, thus depriving itself of independent advice when it was embarking on a wholly new method for a UK university of raising loan support for a capital programme. The strength of an external team is its independence and the confidence this may give to an audit committee – clearly the case at Portsmouth – but for routine internal audit work such as compiling reports on departmental budget practice it lacks the organizational familiarity which can enable internal audit to make such an important contribution to institutional management. The larger university the stronger is the case for appointing an internal team.

Managing the audit committee processes can be internally stressful when implicitly the committee's position must be to question the university's senior officers, including the vice-chancellor, on the processes employed to run the university. The internal auditor, whether an internal appointment or a member of an outside organization, should normally be the secretary of the committee (acting, if necessary, under delegated authority from the registrar) to ensure independence. The committee needs to be closely involved in the appointment of the internal auditor and to approve his/her schedule of work so that it keeps unfettered control of the key processes. Senior officers should attend its meetings by invitation only, and should not be present when the committee has its meeting with the external auditors. The committee, however, should have no executive powers; executive action should be initiated by recommendations to the governing body or to the vice-chancellor; questions of disciplinary action arising from the committee's findings should always be handled elsewhere, through the institution's normal disciplinary processes, and never by the committee itself (as at Portsmouth). Audit processes are not designed to be popular but the committee needs to bear in mind that it will succeed best if it provides clear explanations of the processes it follows and is seen to be acting in the interests of the institution rather than as an external enforcement agency.

Remuneration committee

The role of remuneration committees is becoming increasingly sensitive publicly as the gap between vice-chancellors' pay and the average pay of the academic community widens. Remuneration committees, however, may cover the salaries of a range of other senior staff as well. Universities will vary in their practice in handling professorial salaries where these are not tied to established scales. Most will delegate this to a special committee chaired by the vice-chancellor which has academic as well as lay membership which has the expertise to review academic performance. It is good practice, however, for this committee to have its recommendations endorsed by the remuneration committee and not simply to operate as an advisory body to the vice-chancellor so as to protect the vice-chancellor from accusations of prejudice or favouritism. The remuneration committee itself should comprise the chair of the governing body, the chair of the finance committee and such other lay members as are considered necessary, together with the vice-chancellor who, however, should not be a member when his/her own salary is considered. The secretary of the committee should be the secretary to the governing body.

The requirement that a vice-chancellor's emoluments should be set out in the institution's accounts together with the numbers of staff paid more than £70,000 was intended to increase public ac-countability but does not seem to have been effective in controlling an escalation of salaries. A remuneration committee ought always, in addition to drawing on the CUC's comparative salary data base, to commission a statement of salary movement in its own institution in order to provide a context for the consideration of senior salaries. It should also draw on the results of performance reviews (see above) and on the annual performance monitoring conducted by the chair in relation to the vice-chancellor, and by the vice-chancellor in re-lation to other senior staff. Obtaining assessments of performance on a 360-degree basis, while often difficult in a university context, can provide a remuneration committee with a broader perspective and can serve as a safeguard in a situation where salaries have necessarily to be determined by a very small group. Remuneration committees are wise to lay down formal pay review cycles, of perhaps two or three years, so as to avoid the inflationary pressures of considering merit, as distinct from inflation-linked salary awards every year.

The principle of formal reporting to the governing body has been established, both for salary awards and, after Huddersfield, for se-verance arrangements. How this is done, and in what detail, is a matter for the governing body, not the remuneration committee, to determine, but a good principle should be that the report should contain an account of the process adopted so that the governing body can itself be assured and can if necessary ensure external ac-countability, of the factors taken into account and the broad basis of the judgements in individual cases.

Nominations committee   ∎

The above accounts of the requirements for the successful operation of the audit and remuneration committees illustrate very clearly the importance of attracting people of an appropriate calibre and experience to the membership of governing bodies. Conventional wisdom suggests that governing bodies and nomination committees should identify key skills which the governing body should seek to have in its representation, in addition to gender and ethnic balance, but personal factors cannot be ignored or a governing body will find itself unable to rely on the judgement of its committees in dealing with sensitive issues. Attracting appropriate people to membership of governing bodies is an increasingly difficult task as the demands on membership with calls for greater accountability grow. In the private sector, as we have seen above, companies are using head hunters and increased financial rewards to identify non-executive members of boards, and universities could find themselves in a similar situation. It has become common to advertise membership vacancies as a way of obtaining greater diversity of membership but experience has been mixed and there seems to be no substitute for nominations committees committing themselves to running recruitment exercises, irrespective of whether actual vacancies have arisen and, having identified potential members, persuading them to come on to the committees as a way of building up a stock of people from whom governing body membership vacancies can be filled. This practice has the advantage of establishing what sort of contribution a person might make and whether they have the time available to take on the responsibilities required.

The difficulty in finding members should not be allowed to turn the nominations committee into a decision-making body on behalf of the governing body. Membership of the committee should reflect the membership of the governing body and should always include senior academic members; discussion of areas of expertise required on the governing body should be initiated at the governing body and names eventually brought forward by the committee should be voted on in a ballot in order to ensure that each nomination wins the positive support of more than 50 per cent of the members present and voting. In addition to curriculum vitae, the chair should introduce each name with the reasons for the nomination to ensure that the governing body as a whole feels that it has fully participated in the decision.

Induction of new members ▮

The CUC has established a 'governor development' programme (now managed by the Leadership Foundation) which includes a special programme for new members of governing bodies and, as a matter of course, institutions should have induction events as well. Almost no institutions offer induction programmes for new members of senates/academic bodies or of faculty boards although similar considerations apply. Members who are not familiar with the powers of the bodies they serve on or the procedures within which they work are less able to contribute and are less able to carry out the responsibilities which membership requires. Better educated committees make better decisions, more quickly, whether a governing body or any other decision-making body in a university; we need to take governance seriously and professionally at all levels and not just at the governing body.

Induction programmes need not be heavy-handed events but at minimum new members should have explained to them by the chair and secretary their responsibilities as members, the context in which the body is operating, including the agreed institutional strategic and financial plans, and the body's procedures, sub-committee structures and modes of conducting business. The investment of time and effort at this early stage will be repaid by much more committed membership when difficult decisions have to be taken by the body concerned.

Joint committees ▮

The most positive, and least contentious, of the Jarratt Committee recommendations was for the creation of a joint governing body/ senate planning and resources committees to be chaired by the vice-chancellor. Many pre-1992 universities have translated this into an explicit strategy committee leaving the detail of internal resource allocation between academic areas to be decided elsewhere. From a governance point of view the strength of the joint committee approach in regard to strategy is the bringing together of long-term academic, financial and property considerations in one body and the binding together of lay and academic views on strategic issues, facilitated further by the fact that both the senate and the council might be expected to discuss the committee's reports. Historically, the pre-1992 universities have used joint committee approaches for other issues, the most obvious being in relation to student employment (careers advisory boards) or on human resource issues, most notably pensions. Such approaches have been much less evident amongst the post-1992 HECs where the separation of governing body and academic board business has been sharper. However, the CUC governance survey (CUC 2000) threw up evidence that some HECs were recognizing the shortcomings of too great a separation of business and were experimenting with joint governing body/academic board conferences and a better articulation of governing body and academic board business.

Experience suggests that joint committees in relevant areas build confidence and mutual respect, as well as bringing together mutually reinforcing expertise. A corollary of the joint committee approach is that reports go for discussion to both bodies, even though final decisions are the prerogative of only one of them. Universities which have a clearly identified central management group, as Lambert found at Warwick and Strathclyde, would naturally field that group, or a subset of it, onto a joint committee on strategy, just as the governing body would nominate its own senior and engaged members, so that the membership was expert and could be expected to carry their respective bodies on controversial issues.

Terms of reference, delegation and standing orders

Effective governance depends in part on a common understanding within the university of process and procedure: a committee can or cannot take a decision; it has or it has not been given delegated powers; the business is within or not within its remit; if votes have to be taken a motion must or must not be seconded and must be spelled out before it is put to the meeting not simply decided on a show of hands with no one sure what they have voted for. At the heart of some of the problems at Lancaster was that there was uncertainty about what powers had been delegated to the finance and general purposes committee and how they should be exercised when speedy decision-making was required and how committees could be kept informed of related decision-making which had financial consequences. Every committee, at whatever level in the governance structure, should have terms of reference given to it by its superior body which should include a statement as to whether that body has delegated powers in what areas of business and in what instances a chair can act for the committee and under what reporting back requirements. Audit committees should insist that a statement of delegations be drawn up for its consideration. Standard authorities on the law of meetings (Farrington 1994, Palfreyman 1998) describe the basic rules for the conduct of meetings which will not be repeated here, except to emphasize that all statutory bodies should have standing orders which set out the way business is conducted, including quorum rules and procedures for moving motions and amendments and for voting. Standing orders provide an essential framework for the conduct of university business: ignored and unconsulted in routine business they provide the necessary tool kit when internal crises occur which enables issues to be decided in a regulated and equitable manner.

Agendas and minutes

The preparation of papers for meetings and the construction of minutes are critical to the orderly conduct of business. Together these represent not just the material on which members prepare themselves prior to a meeting and the record of the decisions taken, but also the basis on which recommendations are made to higher bodies and the permanent record of the process which can be referred to for information at any time in the future by readers not necessarily familiar with the business. This transparency is essential if committee papers like those of the governing body or senate/academic board are circulated for information on the university's website or deposited for reading in the library.

Agendas which have papers attached to each item need to identify the papers so that they can be referred to in minutes and traced to explain the background to the decision. Items which report back decisions from a higher body should quote the precise minute recording the decision not some abbreviated version so that any caveats or conditions can be understood. In appropriate circumstances it can be good practice to indicate on the agenda an intention to allot a specified time to discussion of a particular complex item so as to warn members in advance of its importance or to indicate that an item is placed on the agenda for a longer term open-ended strategic discussion, on which it is not planned to reach a conclusion at that meeting. On statutory body agendas where a significant number of routine approvals may be sought, the agenda may be divided up into matters which require discussion and matters that will be passed on the nod unless any member wishes to question them. These devices signpost the conduct of committee business for members who may not be closely involved in all the business and enable them to prepare themselves better for key issues.

Committees are about action and they should meet to take decisions not to obfuscate business and prevaricate: their minutes should therefore be brief and should record what was considered and what decided, including records of voting figures etc., if issues were decided in this way; minutes which contain lengthy records of discussion can be used to reopen consideration at the next meeting and can be endlessly challenged as to whether they convey all the nuances of the previous debate. A minute can represent the final authority for executive action and should therefore be drafted with implementation in mind. The institution is not helped if a wording is such that it allows no flexibility if circumstances change between meetings.

Minutes need to be drafted quickly after the meeting and it is a good rule that approvals from the chair should be obtained within a week of the meeting taking place. This enables implementation to be immediate and where resolutions or recommendations need to be passed to other bodies the conduct of business by these bodies is not delayed. Of course where a body like a senior management team or inner cabinet meets weekly the operation of minuting and passing on decisions has to be reduced to two or three days. Crispness in the processing of committee decisions has a considerable impact on the effectiveness of governance as a whole. This sets a requirement for an efficient 'academic civil service' which can manage the process of governance, give policy and procedural advice to committees, as appropriate, and ensure that the decision-making wheels move at a sufficient pace. A key element in this is trust – trust in the committee process, trust in the integrity of the 'academic civil service', and trust in the efficacy of the governance structure as a whole. Where trust breaks down, where committee decisions are distorted or overridden, minutes flawed, implementation patchy, governance itself suffers. The Cardiff, Lancaster and Cambridge stories would all have been different if a robust committee secretariat had been able to ensure due process – that sinking funds were established when it was agreed they should be, that minutes were drafted, circulated to the right people and implemented and that warnings, legitimately made, were listened to. Effective, efficient committee 'servicing' builds trust in a university's decision-making processes and forms a crucial component of good governance.

Good governance is in part the product of good working relationships between the chair of a committee and its secretary when both are intent on forwarding the interests of the body they serve. The chair has the task of controlling the meeting, working with members to reach decisions and ensuring that those decisions are taken in a proper manner reflecting the evidence placed before the meeting. The secretary, in addition to providing policy advice as required, must be the master of procedure and of ensuring that adequate material is circulated beforehand in a usable form and that decisions are properly recorded and implemented. This is not simply a requirement for governing bodies, but for senates/academic boards and faculty boards, departmental meetings and examination boards in departments. Good governance is dependent on good practice, on professionalism on the part of the chair, the secretary and the members. Governance breaks down when common understandings about the importance of structure, process and open debate are outweighed by the pressure of events, the particularity or dominance of individuals or groups, or by the apathy of members. University governance demands commitment from all the parties involved to be effective.

Conflicts of interest

The routines of the compilation of a register of interests for members of governing bodies have been the norm in universities since the setting up of the Nolan Committee. In practice, such a register, while important as the recognition of a principle, has not had any great operational impact because it is rare, under current arrangements, for governing body members to have commercial relationships with the university with which they are associated. Conflicts of interest are, in fact, much more likely to exist in other areas of governance. The CUC *Guide* emphasizes the point that: 'Members nominated by particular constituencies should not act as if delegated by the group they represent' (CUC 2004). This is important in respect to student and staff members, at any governance level (though governing bodies and senates/academic boards are often flexible for internal political reasons in conceding the legitimacy of student contributions which reflect immediate and local student interests).

In academic governance, issues of conflict of interest arise very easily – departments within one faculty will support issues of interest to their own faculty over the interests of other faculties, members of departments can be more sympathetic to the interests of departmental colleagues than to others, personal relationships, of which colleagues are not aware, may introduce conflicts of interest which obscure academic or professional judgements. At one level, for example in respect to judgements about individuals or to resource allocation issues, these conflicts can be dealt with by requiring departmental colleagues to leave the room while decisions are discussed and concluded. This demonstrates an important principle about the need for fairness and transparency in university decision-making. The question of the declaration of personal relationships is more difficult to resolve because they may be transitory or only relevant in some circumstances and not in others. Nevertheless a principle needs to be established and made part of the organizational culture that members of staff disqualify themselves from taking, or participate in taking, decisions in which they may have a personal interest. Chairs of committees can help this principle to be observed by routinely asking at the beginning of meetings for any declarations of personal interest to be made.

9

PRESSURES FOR CHANGE IN UNIVERSITY GOVERNANCE

The last decade has seen unprecedented pressures for change in university governance. Beginning with the Jarratt Report which sought *inter alia* to reinvigorate the roles of university governing bodies to the 1992 legislation which created a whole tranche of new universities with HEC constitutions and to the subsequent recommendations of the Dearing Committee on governance through to the Lambert Report, we have seen a steady trend to push the university sector towards a more corporate model. In one sense this rests on the unfounded proposition that the appropriate analogy for university governing bodies is the company board. In an earlier period when political attitudes were different, if change had been sought a style of governance more appropriate to the non-profit sector might have been espoused. In practice, universities are eleemosynary corporations, and, as such, exempt charities, whose form of governance is *sui generis* and necessarily so because their business is different and distinct from the corporate and non-profit sectors. The pressures towards the corporate model have been reinforced by the much greater concern for accountability, arising first out of the Cardiff affair and then from the introduction of a much more regulated environment in the corporate sector.

Within universities the creation of central management boards or steering committees to better coordinate and accelerate decision-making and the widespread devolution of decision-making in key financial areas to faculties have had a substantial impact on internal governance processes, and reflects a view that 'modernized' governance structures make a significant contribution to performance. Many of these internal changes are a response to the demand for a quicker reaction time to external pressures, and their actual contribution to the more successful prosecution of the core business of teaching and research is unproven. The response of University E in Chapter 6 to these external pressures might suggest that some reversion from heavily devolved to more centralized structures could be a theme for the next decade. Meanwhile, the establishment of more 'business-like' structures at major universities like Imperial College and the University of Manchester could prove to be trend setters or could come to be seen as experiments that did not justify the organizational upheavals that they provoked. We have no research evidence in the corporate world that improvements in company performance can be associated with changes in corporate governance although it goes without saying that, as in the case of TransTec, ineffective corporate governance can bring companies to disaster.

In my 'Review of university management and governance at Cambridge arising out of the Capsa project' (Shattock 2001), I picked out for critical comment a sentence in an introduction to Cornford's *Microsmographica Academic*: 'We are still, many say governed "very badly" but that does not seem to affect the University's capacity to achieve academic distinction' (Johnson 1994). In the context of the attitudes in some parts of the University to the Capsa findings a critical comment was defensible but the phrase nevertheless contains a wider truth. If we are to believe the world rankings that have emerged from the Shanghai Jiao Tong University and from the *Times Higher Education Supplement* university league tables, changes in governance structures at Oxbridge need to be argued for on grounds other than that the current forms have damaged academic performance since these two universities are clearly 'world class', a condition which only a few UK universities can realistically claim for themselves. Good governance in universities is clearly important both as a matter of public policy and to ensure that academic self-governance works for the benefit of members of the institution and contributes to achieving institutional objectives. But simply because the governance structures at Oxford and Cambridge are different does not mean that their academic performance would be improved by bringing them into line with civic university or even HEC constitutions. The preponderance of 'world-class' universities are in the US and it is in these universities where shared governance and the key influence of the faculty in governance is most in evidence.

Reducing the size of university governing bodies, for example, may or may not, depending on the university's context and decision-making culture, represent an improvement in governance but it is unlikely to contribute much to the academic business of the university unless it has been driven by real internal arguments for a new structure. In considering the pressures for change in governance practice universities should be careful to weigh them against the key objectives and mission of the institution. There is evidence of some convergence between the civic university and HEC models, as the pre-1992 universities adjust their governing body membership to the CUC Code's recommendation of 25. Perhaps of more significance is that some pre-1992 governing bodies are beginning to flex their muscles along the lines provided for under HEC constitions. The longer term impact of this on success in the core business of teaching and research is difficult to predict. External pressures may be valuable in highlighting weaknesses and the need for change but if they come with some kind of official imprimatur or are simply the result of 'me-too-ism' they may also have the effect of reducing institutional differentiation, weakening autonomy, or damaging academic morale. Similarly, costly changes, in terms of time and energy, in academic governance structures, will not themselves guarantee improved performance, which will only come about through addressing academic problems at their roots which lie in the disciplines, course programmes and departments.

The last decade has seen a plethora of academic governance re-organizations driven by the external pressures described in Chapter 5. It is likely this process will continue, facilitated by the greater powers of initiation that present governance structures now accord vice-chancellors and governing bodies. Such changes need to be monitored with care because restructuring can be a panacea for rectifying perceived institutional shortcomings. Too often the investment of time and energy in changing governance structures can be a distraction from dealing with the real issues of academic departments that need strengthening, buildings that need modernizing or management processes that need reform. Restructuring, in fact, is the easy bit; the task of institutional improvement is more likely to be a long haul requiring a constant managerial attention to the detail of making better appointments, redirecting budget priorities and setting ever more demanding institutional targets.

The consequences of governance changes for the involvement of individual members of the academic community in the life of the institution is more difficult to assess. As universities have got bigger it is inevitable that individuals find themselves pushed further away from the decision-making process. The concerned, public spirited, academic who contributed at all sorts of governance levels in the past is more likely to be replaced by the RAE-driven academic or the over-pressed university teacher too busy to participate in bodies which seem to be a long way from the action. Why bother to sit on a senate or academic board when the critical policy debates are taking place within the vice-chancellor's executive committee? Undoubtedly, this represents a loss to the system and holds dangers for the future in the possible alienation of the staff from the core objectives of the institution. Universities need to do all in their power to engage the interest and enthusiasm of their staff, not least because they represent the seed corn for future heads of departments, deans, pro-vice-chancellors and ultimately vice-chancellors, but mainly because the evidence suggests that universities are better run the more their staff are fully engaged with the pressures that confront them.

Paradoxically, considering the position of staff, one change that may occur as a result of the 2006 rise in student fees and the implementation of the National Student Attitudes Survey is a welcome resurgence of student interest in university governance. For the last quarter of a century the student contribution at governing bodies and senates/academic boards has mostly been minimal except on strictly local and transitory issues. While it is unlikely that the new marketization will release consumerism in a conventional sense it would be surprising if student representatives and student unions did not adopt a new involvement in the conduct of teaching and that this was not translated into a greater engagement with institutional decision-making across a broad area of university governance.

Universities need good governance to survive in a changing and more marketized environment. They have complex governance structures which reflect their complex organizational structures, which can be made to seem, and often are, sluggish and self-defeating. On the other hand, when they work well they confer great benefit on the institution concerned. But making them work well demands vigilance, transparency and a significant investment in time and resources. The greatest threat to shared governance is that the academic community becomes no longer willing to invest in making it work.

REFERENCES

Aitken, R. (1966) *Administration of a University*. London: University of London Press page 77.

Aldous, H. and Kaye, R. (2003) *TransTec plc: Investigation under Section 432 (2) of the Companies Act 1985*. Department of Trade and Industry, London: The Stationery Office.

Aldous and Kaye *ibid* a para 5.16.

Aldous and Kaye *ibid* b para 5.17.

Aldous and Kaye *ibid* c para 5.176.

Aldous and Kaye *ibid* d para 5.53.

Ashby, E. (1963) *Technology and the Academics*. London: Macmillan.

Ashby *ibid* a page 71.

Ashby *ibid* b page 73.

Ashby *ibid* c page 72.

Ashby, E. and Anderson, M. (1970) *The Rise of the Student Estate in Britain*. London: Macmillan.

Austin, D. (1982) 'Salva sit universitas nostra: a memoir', *Government and Opposition*. Vol. 17 pages 469–89.

Bargh, C., Scott, P. and Smith, D. (1996) *Governing Universities: Changing the Culture?* Buckingham: Open University Press.

Bargh, C., Bocock, J., Smith, D. and Scott, P. (2000) *University Leadership. The Role of the Chief Executive*. Buckingham: Open University Press a pages 26–36.

Bargh *et al ibid* b page 154.

Bargh *et al ibid* c page 160.

Bargh *et al ibid* d page 157.

Becher, T. and Kogan, M. (1992) *Process and Structure in Higher Education*. London: Routledge.

Becher and Kogan *ibid* a page 81.

Bennett, B. (2002) 'The new style of boards – are they working?', *Higher Education Quarterly*. Vol. 56 No. 3.

Berdahl, R.O. (1959) *British Universities and the State*. Berkeley, CA: University of California Press.

Birnbaum, R. (2000) *Management Fads in Higher Education*. San Francisco: Jossey Bass.

Bolton, A. (2000) *Managing the Academic Unit*. Buckingham: Open University Press.

Bolton *ibid* page 12.

Braun, D. and Merrien F-X (1999) *Towards a New Model of Governance for Universities. A Comparative View*. London: Jessica Kingsley Publishers.

Brown, R. (2003) 'Southampton Institute' in Warner, D. and Palfreyman, D. (eds) *Managing Crisis*. Maidenhead Open University Press a page 58.

Brown *ibid* b page 60.

Brown *ibid* c page 60.

Buckland, R. (2004) 'Universities and industry: Does the Lambert Code of Governance meet the requirements of good governance?', *Higher Education Quarterly*. Vol. 58 No. 4.

Burgess, K. (2005) 'Low level of compliance with new governance code', *Financial Times* 12 October, page 2.

Butler, the Lord (2004) *Review of Intelligence on Weapons of Mass Destruction*. Report of a Committee of Privy Counsellors, Chairman the Lord Butler. HC 898 London: The Stationery Office para. 6.11.

Cadbury, A. (1992) *Report of the Committee on the Financial Aspects of Corporate Governance* (the Cadbury Report). London: London Stock Exchange.

Cadbury *ibid* a para. 4.9.

Cadbury *ibid* b para. 4.11.

Cadbury *ibid* c para. 2.5.

Caulkin, S. (2005) 'Boards cannot focus on strategy if they're forever box ticking', *Observer Business* 27 November.

Chait, R., Holland, T.P. and Taylor, B.E. (1991) *The Effective Board of Trustees*. New York ACE/MacMillan; Phoenix AZ: ACE/Onyx second edition 1993.

Chait, Holland and Taylor *ibid* a Introduction.

Chait, R.P., Holland, T.P. and Taylor, B.E. (1996) *Improving the Performance of Governing Boards*. Phoenix, AZ: ACE/Onyx a page 1.

Chait, Holland and Taylor *ibid* b page 3.

Chait, Holland and Taylor *ibid* c page 4.

Chait, Holland and Taylor *ibid* d page 7.

Chesterman, M. (1979) *Charities, Trusts and Social Welfare*. London: Weidenfeld & Nicolson.

Clark, B.R. (1998) *Creating Entrepreneurial Universities. Organisational Pathways of Transformation*. Oxford: Pergammon.

Commission of Inquiry (the North Report) (1997) *Commission of Inquiry Supplementary Volume*. Oxford: University of Oxford Press, a page 90.

Commission of Inquiry *ibid* b page 21.

Commission of Inquiry *ibid* c page 18.

Committee of Public Accounts (1990) *Financial Problems at Universities First Report*. London: HMSO 15 January a para. 15.

Committee of Public Accounts *ibid* b. Memorandum submitted by Permanent Secretary, Department of Education and Science para. 28.

Committee of Public Accounts (1995) *Severance Payments to Senior Staff in the Publicly Funded Education Sector.* Minutes of Evidence HC 242–1 1994–95 London: HMSO.

Committee of Vice-Chancellors and Principals (1985) *Report of the Steering Committee for Efficiency Studies in Universities* (Jarratt Report) London: CVCP March a page 8.

Committee of Vice-Chancellors and Principals *ibid* b page 24.

Committee of Vice-Chancellors and Principals *ibid* c page 22.

Committee of Vice-Chancellors and Principals *ibid* d page 24.

Committee of Vice-Chancellors and Principals *ibid* e page 26.

Committee on Higher Education (the Robbins Committee) (1963) *Higher Education Report.* London: HMSO Cmnd. 2154 para 676.

Committee on Standards in Public Life (the Nolan Committee) (1996) *Local Public Spending Bodies Summary of the Committee's Second Report.* London: HMSO page 3.

Cornforth, C. (ed.) (2003) *The Governance of Public and Non-Profit Organisations.* London: Routledge.

Croham Report (1987) *Review of the University Grants Committee. Report of a Committee under the Chairmanship of Lord Croham.* London: HMSO cm. 81.

CUC (1995) *Guide for Members of Governing Bodies of Universities and Colleges in England, Wales and Northern Ireland.* London: CUC/HEFCE.

CUC (1998) *Guide for Members of Governing Bodies of Universities and Colleges in England, Wales and Northern Ireland.* London: CUC/HEFCE.

CUC (2000) *Guide for Members of Governing Bodies of Universities and Colleges in England, Wales and Northern Ireland.* London: CUC/HEFCE December para 3.17.

CUC *ibid* a page 1.

CUC *ibid* b *Review of University Governance 1997–2000.*

CUC (2004) *Guide for Members of Higher Education Governing Bodies in the UK.* London: CUC/HEFCE November 2004/40.

CUC *ibid* a para. 218.

CUC *ibid* b page 11.

CUC *ibid* c page 19.

CUC *ibid* d Governance Code of Practice para. 1.

CUC *ibid* e pages 127–129.

CUC *ibid* f page 15.

Deem, R. (1998) 'New managerialism and higher education: the management of performance and cultures in universities in the United Kingdom', *International Studies in Sociology of Education* Vol. 8 No. 1 pages 47–70.

Department for Education and Skills (Rt. Hon. Charles Clarke) (2003) 'Higher education funding and delivery to 2005–6'. Letter to Mr. David Young, Chairman, HEFCE 22 January.

Department for Education and Skills (2003) *The Future of Higher Education.* CM 5735 London: The Stationery Office.

Durham, K. (1982) 'Foreword' in Oldham, G. (ed.) *The Future of Research.* Leverhulme Programme of Study into the Future of Higher Education. London: Society for Research into Higher Education.

Duryea, E.D. (2000) *The Academic Corporation. A History of College and University Governing Boards.* London: Falmer Press.

Ehrenberg, R.G. (2002) *Tuition Rising. Why College Costs so Much.* Cambridge, MA: Harvard University Press page 22.

Farrington, D.J. (1994) *The Law of Higher Education.* London: Butterworths.

Foster, J.M. (2002) 'Enron – The story to date'. Paper to the Conference on Enron and Auditor Independence; the implications for the UK. One Whitehall Place, 26 April.

Green, V.H.H. (1969) *The Universities.* Harmondsworth: Penguin Books.

Greenbury, R. (1995) *Director's Remuneration: A Report of a Study Group chaired by Sir Richard Greenbury.* London: Gee Publishing.

Greenspan, A. (2002) 'Infectious greed', *Financial Times* 20 July.

Hampel, R. (1998) *Committee on Corporate Governance, Final Report* (the Hampel Report). London: Gee Publishing.

Hampel *ibid* a para 1.2.

Hampel *ibid* b para 1.14.

Hampel *ibid* c para 1.11.

Hampel *ibid* d para 1.12.

Hampel, R. (2003) 'Box ticking is bad for business', *Financial Times* 15 May.

HEFCE (2000) *Model Financial Memorandum between the HEFCE and Institutions.* HEFCE 0025 a para. 56d.

HEFCE *ibid* b para. 12.

HEFCE *ibid* c para. 18.

HEFCE *ibid* d para. 19.

HEFCE (2004) *Accountability and Audit: HEFCE Code of Practice.* London: HEFCE a 2004/27 para. 19.

HEFCE *ibid* b para. 22.

HEFCE *ibid* c para. 23.

HEFCE *ibid* d para. 73.

Higgs, D. (2003) *Review of the Role and Effectiveness of Non-Executive Directors.* London: HMSO.

Hoeveler, J.D. (1981) *James McCosh and the Scottish Intellectual Tradition.* Princeton, NJ: Princeton University Press.

Hofstadter, R. (1955) *Academic Freedom in the Age of the College.* New York: Columbia University Press a page 237.

Hofstadter *ibid* b page 238.

Hofstadter *ibid* c page 274.

Hogan, J. (2005) 'Should form follow function? Changing academic structures in UK universities', *Perspectives.* Vol. 9 No. 2 pages 49–57.

Hogan *ibid* a page 53.

Hogan *ibid* b page 53.

Hogan *ibid* c page 53.

Hogan *ibid* d page 54.

Hogan *ibid* e page 54.

Holland, T.P. (1991) 'Self assessment by non-profit boards', *Non Profit Management and Leadership.* Vol. 2 No. 1 pages 25–36.

Holmes, D.R. (1998) 'Some personal reflections on the role of administrators and managers in British Universities', *Perspectives*. Vol. 2 No. 4 pages 110–117 a page 112.

Holmes *ibid* b page 112.

Ives, E., Drummond, D. and Schwartz, L. (2000) *The First Civic University: Birmingham 1880–1980*. Birmingham: University of Birmingham Press.

Jarzabkowski, P. (2002) 'Centralised or decentralised? Strategic implications of resource allocation models', *Higher Education Quarterly*. Vol. 56 No. 1 pages 5–32.

Johnson, G. (1994) *University Politics. F.M. Cornford's Cambridge and his Advice to the Young Academic Politician*. Cambridge: Cambridge University Press page 83.

Jones, S. and Kiloh, G. (1987) 'The management of polytechnics and colleges' in Becher, R.A. (ed) *British Higher Education*. London: Allen & Unwin.

Karp, A. and Duryea (1979) 'English antecedents to the corporate form of government in American colleges and universities'. Paper presented to Association for Study of Higher Education, quoted in Duryea, E.D. (2000) *The Academic Corporation, A History of College and University Governing Boards*. London: Falmer Press page 83.

Keasey, K., Thompson, S. and Wright, M. (1997) *Corporate Governance: Economic, Management and Financial Issues*. Oxford: OUP.

Kerr, C. (2001) *The Gold and the Blue*. Berkeley and Los Angeles: University of California Press page 221.

Kerr, C. and Glade, M.L. (1989) *The Guardians Boards of Trustees of American Colleges and Universities, What they Do and How Well they Do it*. Washington: Association of Governing Boards of Universities and Colleges.

Kerr and Glade *ibid* a page 139.

Knight, M. (2002) 'Governance in higher education corporations: a consideration of the constitution created by the 1992 Act', *Higher Education Quarterly*. Vol. 56 No. 3 July.

Kwickers, P. (2005) 'Governing governance: organisation law and network – process – design', *International Journal for Education Law and Policy*. Vol. 1 Issue 1–2 pages 73–102.

Lambert, R. (2003) *Lambert Review of Business – University Collaboration Final Report*. London: HMSO.

Lambert *ibid* a para. 7.3.

Lambert *ibid* b para. 7.6.

Lambert *ibid* c para. 1.11.

Lambert *ibid* d para. 7.21.

Lambert *ibid* e para. 7.7.

Lambert *ibid* f para. 7.11.

Lambert *ibid* g para. 7.2.

McClintoch, M. and Ritchie, W. (2003) 'Capital building and cash flow at the University of Lancaster' in Warner, D. and Palfreyman, D. (2003) *Managing Crisis*. Maidenhead: Open University Press.

McFall, J. (2002) 'Scope and purpose of the Treasury Select Committee Inquiry'. Paper to the Conference on Enron and Auditor Independence: the implications for the UK. One Whitehall Place 26 April.

Middlehurst, R. (2004) 'Changing internal governance: a discussion of leadership roles and management structures in UK universities', *Higher Education Quarterly*. Vol. 58, No. 4 pages 258–280.

Moodie, G.C. and Eustace, R.B. (1974) *Power and Authority in British Universities*. London: Allen & Unwin.

Moodie and Eustace *ibid* a page 34.

Moodie and Eustace *ibid* b page 34.

Moodie and Eustace *ibid* c page 36.

Moodie and Eustace *ibid* d page 233.

Moodie and Eustace *ibid* e see Chapter IV pages 58–90.

Muth, M.M. and Donaldson, L. (1998) 'Stewardship theory and board structure: a contingency approach', *Corporate Governance*. Vol. 6 No. 1.

NAB (National Advisory Body for Public Sector Higher Education) (1987) *Management for a Purpose. The Report of the Good Management Practice Group*. NAB: London March.

NAO (National Audit Office) (1995) *Severance Payments to Senior Staff in the Publicly Funded Sector*. HC 202 Session 1994–95 London: HMSO 10 February.

NAO *ibid* a page 21.

NAO *ibid* b page 76.

NAO *ibid* c page 76.

NAO *ibid* d page 77.

NAO (National Audit Office) (1998) *The Management of Building Projects at English Higher Education Institutions*, HC 452 Session 1997–98 16 January. London: HMSO.

NAO (National Audit Office) (1998) *Overseas Operations, Governance and Management at Southampton Institute*. HC 23 Session 1998–99 London: The Stationery Office 11 December a page 75.

NCIHE (National Committee of Inquiry into Higher Education) (the Dearing Report) (1977) *Higher Education in the Learning Society*. London: HMSO a para. 15.33.

NCIHE *ibid* b para. 15.48.

NCIHE *ibid* c para. 15.37.

NCIHE *ibid* d para. 15.38.

OECD (1998) *Corporate Governance. Improving Competitiveness and Access to Capital in Global Markets* Paris: OECD April page 17.

Palfreyman, D. (1998) 'The law of meetings' in Palfreyman, D. and Warner, D. *Higher Education and the Law*. Buckingham: Open University Press.

Plender, J. (2005) 'Companies facing regulatory fatigue', *Financial Times* 10 March.

Pratt, J. (1997) *The Polytechnic Experiment 1965–92*. Buckingham: Open University Press page 29.

Pullen, B. with Abendstern, M. (2004) *A History of the University of Manchester 1973–90*. Manchester: Manchester University Press a page 55.

Pullen *ibid* b page 55.

Pullen *ibid* c page 55.

Rashdall, H. (1936) *The Universities of Europe in the Middle Ages*. (Powicke, F.M. and Emden, A.B. (eds)). Oxford: Oxford University Press Vol. III page 49.

Roberts, D. (2004) 'The boardroom burden: calls for reform are replaced by concern that corporate shake-up has gone too far', *Financial Times* 1 June.

Rowe, P. (ed) (1997) *The University of Lancaster: Review of Institutional Lessons to be Learned 1994–1996*. Lancaster: The University of Lancaster Press.
Rowe *ibid* a page 205.
Rowe *ibid* b page 205.
Rowe *ibid* c page 219.
Rowe *ibid* d page 43.
Rowe *ibid* e page 38.
Rowe *ibid* f page 91.
Rowe *ibid* g page 92.
Rowe *ibid* h page 54.
Rowe *ibid* i page 245.
Rowe *ibid* j page 207.
Ruegg, W. (1992) 'Themes' in De Ridder-Symoens, H. (ed.) *A History of the University in Europe. Volume 1. Universities in the Middle Ages*. Cambridge: CUP page 238.
Salter, B. and Tapper, T. (2002) 'The external pressures on the internal governance of universities', *Higher Education Quarterly*. Vol. 56 No. 3.
Scottish Executive (2003) *A Framework for Higher Education in Scotland*. Edinburgh: Scottish Executive.
Shattock, M.L. (1987) *Report on the Implementation of Financial Control at University College, Cardiff* (unpublished) UGC.
Shattock, M.L. (1988) 'Financial management in universities: the lessons from University College, Cardiff', *Financial Management and Accountability*. Vol. 4 No. 2 pages 99–113.
Shattock, M.L. (1994) *The UGC and the Management of British Universities*. Buckingham: Open University Press.
Shattock *ibid* a page 61.
Shattock *ibid* b page 45.
Shattock *ibid* c page 117.
Shattock, M.L. (2001) 'Review of university management and governance issues arising out of the Capsa project', *Cambridge University Reporter*. Vol. CXXXII No. 6 2 November.
Shattock *ibid* a para 5.5.
Shattock *ibid* b para 5.10.
Shattock, M.L. (2002) 'Re-balancing modern concepts of university governance', *Higher Education Quarterly*. Vol. 56 No. 3.
Shattock, M.L. (2003) *Managing Successful Universities*. Maidenhead: Open University Press a page 22.
Shattock *ibid* b pages 147–8.
Shattock *ibid* c pages 103–6.
Shattock, M.L. (2003 d) 'Research, administration and university management: what can research contribute to policy?' in Begg, R. (ed.) *The Dialogue between Higher Education Research and Practice*. Dordrecht: Kluwer Academic Publishers.
Sherman, E. (2005) 'Twist at the end of the rule book', *Financial Times* 21 April.
Shinn, C.H. (1986) *Paying the Paper. The Development of the University Grants Committee 1919–1946*. London: Falmer Press.

Sizer, J. (1987) *Institutional Responses to Financial Reductions in the University Sector, Final Report to the Department of Education and Science*. Loughborough: Loughborough University Press a page 32.

Sizer *ibid* b page 45.

Skapinker, M. (2002) 'The durable practice of partnership' and 'How to harness a myriad of independent minds', *Financial Times* 3 January and 4 January.

Sloman, A.E. (1964) *A University in the Making*. London: BBC Books/University of Oxford.

Smith, B. and Cunningham, V. (2003) 'Crisis in Cardiff' in Warner, D. and Palfreyman, D. (eds) *Managing Crisis*. Maidenhead: Open University Press page 13.

Sonnerfeld, J.A. (2002) 'What makes great boards great?', *Harvard Business Review*. Vol. 80 September pages 106–113.

Taggart, G.J. (2004) *A Critical Review of the Role of the English Funding Body for Higher Education in the Relationship between the State and Higher Education in the Period 1945–2003*. Dissertation submitted for the award of an EdD, University of Bristol a page 42.

Taggart *ibid* b page 2.

Tapper, T. and Salter, B. (1992) *Oxford, Cambridge and the Changing Idea of the University. The Challenge to Donnish Dominion*. Buckingham: Open University Press page 11.

Thorley, H. (1998) 'All those in favour' in Thorley, H. (ed.) *Take a Minute. Reflections on Modern Higher Education Administration*. Lancaster: Unit for Innovation in Higher Education/THES a page 84.

Thorley *ibid* b page 84.

Times Higher Education Supplement (2005) Advertisement, 23 September.

Times Higher Education Supplement (2006) 'Vice-chancellors' pay 2004–05', 10 March

Tricks, H. (2005) 'Search for non-execs leads companies abroad', *Financial Times* 3 October.

Tucker, S. (2004a) 'Non-exec directors' pay up nearly 40%' *Financial Times* 6 December.

Tucker, S. (2004b) 'Patchy performance on Higgs standards', *Financial Times* 26 July.

Tucker, S. (2005) 'Fees for non-executives hit record level after 21% rise', *Financial Times* 18 July.

UGC (1973) Memorandum of General Guidance 15 January.

Universities UK (2004) *Appointing Senior Managers in Higher Education: A Guide to Best Practice*. London: Universities UK.

University of Cambridge (Wass Report) (1989) 'Report of the syndicate appointed to consider the government of the university', *Cambridge University Reporter*. Vol. CXIX No. 26 19 May.

University of Oxford (North Report) (1977) *Commission of Inquiry*. Oxford: OUP.

University of Oxford (Franks Report) (1964) *Report of a Commission of Inquiry and the Chairmanship of Lord Franks*. *Oxford*: OUP a.

University of Oxford *ibid* b para. 551.

University of Warwick (1998–99) *Calendar 1998–99* University of Warwick.
University of Warwick *ibid* a Charter para. 12 page 85.
University of Warwick *ibid* b Charter para. 13 page 85.
University of Warwick *ibid* c Statute 19 para. 98.
University of Warwick *ibid* d Statute 5(4) page 89.
University of Westminster (2005) *Memorandum of Association of the University of Westminster*. Instrument and Articles of Government of the University a para. 3.1.
University of Westminster b para. 8.1.
University of Westminster c para. 11.1.
Watson, D.J. (1989) *Managing the Modular Course*. Buckingham: Open University Press.
Webber, G. (1998) 'Devolved budgeting – challenging the new orthodoxy', *Perspectives*. Vol. 2 No.2 pages 64–69 a page 65.
Webber *ibid* b page 65.
Webber *ibid* c page 65.
Wighton, D. (2004) 'Chaperon watch over Wall St.', *Financial Times* 3 June.
Williams, G. (1992) *Changing Patterns of Finance in Higher Education*. Buckingham: Open University Press.

Index

MANAGING CRISIS

David Warner and David Palfreyman

- Why do crises arise in Further and Higher Education institutions?
- How can these crises be overcome?
- What lessons can be learnt?

There have been several high profile crises in higher education during the last two decades. *Managing Crisis* draws together a number of senior academic managers to prepare, probably for the first time ever, a series of detailed institutional case studies. These case studies identify the nature of the crisis, describe the action taken to resolve it, and consider the lasting consequences. An important chapter gives the informed perspectives of the funding council on higher education crises, and in the final chapter the inimitable Peter Scott draws a series of significant conclusions.

Managing Crisis is the first book to examine crises in higher education in detail and to identify key points on how to overcome or avoid them. Required reading for managers working within UK Higher Education Policy.

Contents: Foreword – Notes on contributors – List of abbreviations – Setting the scene – Crisis at Cardiff – Capital building and cash flow at the University of Lancaster – How one man wove a kind of magic in Ealing – Southampton Institute – The experience of London Guildhall University – Heartbreak ending for a foreign affair – The Lambeth hike – Crisis making and crisis managing – A funding council perspective – Learning the lessons – References – Index.

Contributors:
Roger Brown, Vanessa Cunningham, Chris Duke, Sir Brian Fender, Roderick Floud, Lucy Hodges, Marion McClintock, David Palfreyman, Adrian Perry, William Richie, Peter Scott, Sir Brian Smith, Sir William Taylor, David Warner.

216pp   0 335 21058 9 Paperback   0 335 21059 7 Hardback

MANAGING INSTITUTIONAL SELF-STUDY

David Watson and Elizabeth Maddison

- What is institutional self-study and why is it important for universities and colleges?
- What are its key processes and techniques?
- What can self-study offer institutions for their future success?

Organizational learning is a key concept for complex enterprises at the start of the 21st century and universities and colleges are no exception. However many institutions have been poor at recognising, reacting to and resolving dilemmas raised by changing public and political expectations. This book offers practical guidance, set in the context of theory and with worked examples, showing how disciplined self-study underpins the key decision-making, institutional processes. Moreover, the examples demonstrate that self-study supports the general effectiveness of universities and colleges and leads to improved reputational positioning.

At the heart of the book is the case for the development of the university or college as a mature, self-reflective community, capable of making full use of its analytical and other resources, thereby meeting the internal drive towards evidence-based practice and satisfying the requirements of external agencies. *Managing Institutional Self-Study* is essential reading for higher education managers and policy-makers.

Contents: List of figures and tables – Foreword – Series editors' introduction – Acknowledgements – List of abbreviations – **Part 1: An introduction to institutional self-study** Self-study and organizational learning Self-study in higher education – Self-study: A university perspective – **Part 2: Self-study in action** – The data cycle – The quality cycle – The planning cycle – **Part 3: The uses of self-study** – Self-study and decision-making – Self-study and reputation – An institutional balance sheet – References – Appendix 1: University of Brighton reports and documents – Appendix 2: Websites referred to in the text – Index.

216pp   0 335 21502 5 Paperback   0 335 21503 3 Hardback

MANAGING PEOPLE

Alison Hall

The most important asset of any university or college is its staff, yet the majority of line managers in higher education institutions are not appointed on the basis of their experience of, or expertise in, managing people.

This book is a practical guide to people management for these managers. With contributions from Professor Robin Middlehurst, Tom Kennie and Catherine Simm, Alison Hall guides readers through the employment cycle, from recruitment to parting company, addressing en route those issues that cause line managers to lose most sleep.

Illustrated throughout with case studies and examples of best practice, the book provides a guide to:

- Effective (and legal) recruitment and selection
- Managing the crucial early days of an appointment
- Leadership, team-building, measuring performance and appraisal
- Managing tricky situations such as sickness absence, discipline, stress, harassment and grievances
- Handling the end of an employment relationship fairly

Managing People is essential reading for HE managers, staff in Human Resource departments, consultants and students and staff involved in HR courses.

Contents: Series editors' introduction – Acknowledgements – List of abbreviations – Setting the scene – Managing to get the right person for the job – Managing the early days – Managing for performance today and tomorrow – Managing tricky situations – Managing work-life balance – Managing the termination of employment – References – Index.

216pp   0335209939 Paperback   0335209947 Hardback